the journals of rachel scott

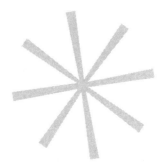

The Journals of

Rachel Scott

A Journey of Faith at Columbine High

Adapted by Beth Nimmo & Debra K. Klingsporn

Tommy nelson
Thomas Nelson, Inc. • Nashville

Published in Nashville, Tennessee, by Tommy Nelson®, a division of Thomas Nelson, Inc.

Scripture quotations used in this book are from *The New Revised Standard Version of the Bible* (NRSV), copyright © 1989 by the Division of Christian Education of the National Council of the Churches of Christ in the USA.

Library of Congress Cataloging-in-Publication Data

Nimmo, Beth.
    The journals of Rachel Scott / [adapted by] Beth Nimmo and Debra K. Klingsporn.
      p. cm.
    ISBN 0-8499-7594-8
    1. Scott, Rachel (Rachel Joy) 2. Christian biography—Colorado. 3. Christian teenagers—Colorado—Biography. 4. High school students—Colorado—Biography. 5. Columbine High School (Littleton, Colo.)—Students—Biography. 6. Christian teenagers—Religious life. I. Scott, Rachel (Rachel Joy) II. Klingsporn, Debra. III. Title.

BR1725.S42 N56 2001
277.3'0829'092—dc21
[B]   00–067879

Printed and bound in the United States of America
04 05 06 BVG 10 9 8 7

contents

Dear Reader,

This book is dedicated to a generation of young people who are searching for what is real and what is true. I believe that search, for many of you, will lead down a spiritual path that eventually directs you toward the Creator. As you explore your spiritual desire, it becomes evident that only God fills the void of our lives. It is God who brings purpose, fulfillment, and meaning to the human soul.

As you read the words of a young girl who was traveling down that path hoping to find her purpose, it is my prayer that you will be inspired to start that spiritual journey.

* * *

When the idea for this book was first conceived, and it was decided that it should be written as if Rachel herself were writing, we knew that the most important element would be choosing the perfect person who could identify with Rachel. In that search, Tommy Nelson recommended Debra Klingsporn. After Debra and I spent several days together sharing our hearts and talking about Rachel, I realized that Debra was a perfect match for this project. She immediately sensed the heart and soul of my daughter, and I knew she would be able to portray Rachel in a true way. I believe Debra was inspired in her writings, as they are very true to the kind of person Rachel was and how she lived her life. Debra has my highest compliments and admiration for the tremendous work she has done.

Beth Nimmo, Rachel Scott's mother

before you start this book—read this!

I'm the writer who was asked to work with Rachel's journals—and you need to know something about who I am, why I was asked to work with Rachel's journals, and how this book came to be.

Assigned the task of trying to "get inside Rachel's head," I was provided with access to everything Rachel had written, said, and e-mailed to those who knew her best. And for the next year, I immersed myself in Rachel's world.

Like Rachel, I began doodling with words when I was barely in my teens. Also like Rachel, by the time I was in high school, I journaled as a way of sorting through my intense range of thoughts and feelings. And most like Rachel, into the pages of my own journals, I wrote impassioned prayers and suicidal thoughts, arguments with myself and questions directed at God, silly observations, trivial musings, and serious reflections. Even once I became fully "adult," I *still* wrote and continue to write into the pages of my journals in these same ways.

Rachel's parents longed to share the raw stuff of their daughter's spiritual journey, a gutsy thing to do. And as I began to read the words Rachel had written on pages of journals, in letters to friends, and in poems and song lyrics scribbled in worn, spiral-bound notebooks, only to be scratched through, revised, and later rewritten into other journals, I found Rachel Joy Scott to be disarmingly honest and painfully real.

The girl I came to know through the words she'd written was a remarkable young woman—not because she was extraordinarily spiritual, talented, or gifted, but because she was so beautifully, honestly, compellingly *real.* Rachel's journals provide a vivid kaleidoscope of a girl's inner life, the raw struggles of an ordinary American teen who hungered for God, had a heart for others, and longed to make a difference in the world.

Ask anyone who knew Rachel to describe her and the replies are quick and consistent. Funny. Dramatic. Persuasive. Charming. Wistful. Engaging. Bright. Witty. Upbeat. Positive. Rachel made people laugh. She made people think. She challenged. She confronted. When she walked into a room, something *changed.* She was like a power charge. Rachel made things come to life.

But for Rachel's parents, making the decision to let her journals be published was not an easy choice. Some of the writings are less than flattering. Some are darkly disturbing. Some entries sound like the words of an upbeat, all-American, well-liked kid. Others sound like words that could have been written by a young woman on the verge of manic depression. How could her family let the radical extremes of her journal entries be made public, yet stay true to the Rachel they knew her to be?

The earliest journal entries found in her room after her death were from the sixth grade. Sometime during that year, she began what her mother calls "friendship journals." Rachel would write a note to a friend in a spiral-bound notebook at school and give it to the friend between classes. That friend would write a response in the notebook and then pass it along to another. And so it would continue through three or four friends before the notebook was passed back to Rachel. Although the friends changed, Rachel continued journal sharing all through high school and had as many as four different friendship journals going simultaneously.

In addition to journals she shared with friends, Rachel kept journals that were intended to be completely private, in which she wrote to God and wrote for herself. Through poems, prayers, random thoughts, doodled drawings, and serious questions, Rachel wrote her life. She wrote as if her feelings were just too big to hold inside, and whether expressing herself in poetry, drama, art, or prose, artistic expression for her was like amplifying the pulse beat of life itself.

Before you read *The Journals of Rachel Scott*, you need to know that reading someone's private journals is to peer inside that person's *most* private self. Thoughts, feelings, perceptions, prayers, and longings that couldn't—or wouldn't—be spoken anywhere else emerge on the pages of a journal.

You also want to know that no private journal gives a complete picture of the person who wrote it. In fact, because journals and diaries are intended to be *private*, the picture they give of an individual is always distorted. Thoreau said, "It is as hard to see oneself as to look backwards without turning around." The person who journals isn't trying to leave a written account of his or her life. Rachel never dreamed someone would gather up all the spiral-bound notebooks, scribbles, drawings, poems, and musings she left laying around her room and put them together for publication.

In her journals, Rachel had an inner dialogue with God, herself, and her closest friends. From the trivial and the silly, to the whining and the unfair, to the lament and the longing, and back again to the profoundly grateful and life-affirming, Rachel's journals are Rachel from the inside out. Rachel's journals are the real stuff of life—and her parents wanted you to benefit from her honesty, her journey, and her struggle. But they also wanted their daughter to be known from the outside in. They wanted her raw honesty and spiritual journey to be published in a way that gave a more complete picture of Rachel Joy Scott. They wanted her charm, wit, humor, intelligence, and bravado to be part of the picture that emerges from the publication of her journals.

So I was asked to write a first-person narrative of Rachel's life, drawing extensively and freely from her journals, but not limiting what I wrote to what was available in those pages. Rachel's mother, Beth Nimmo, opened her heart and her home to me, speaking with honesty, vulnerability, and complete candor about Rachel. Rachel's sisters, Bethanee and Dana, answered questions, provided feedback, and offered insights that only sisters can. And both Rachel's mother and her father, Darrell Scott, showed good humor and humility in their willingness to allow the images that emerge from this narrative to be—at times—less than flattering.

The narrative is based on facts drawn from her journals and from hours of conversation with her family but written as if Rachel herself were telling the story that led her to journaling in the way she did. Her actual entries are provided in her own handwriting, while the first-person narrative was written after carefully studying her journals, praying—and then listening—before putting words on the page.

As an image slowly becomes clear on a connect-the-dot drawing, I pray the picture of Rachel that emerges from the connection of first-person narrative and journal excerpts is true to both who Rachel was—and who she longed to become.

Although the journal entries written by Rachel's friends must remain unpublished out of respect for their privacy, their entries in the shared journals display the huge difference Rachel made in the lives of those who knew her. Both spiritual leader and trusted confidante, Rachel made a difference in the lives of her friends; she made a difference in the lives of her classmates; she made a difference in the lives of her parents and siblings.

Rachel Joy Scott was a life-giving, faith-affirming, compellingly honest girl who wanted to make a difference, who wanted her life to *matter.* The seventeen-year journey of this young woman ended at Columbine High School on April 20, 1999. In making the difficult decision to allow her journals to be published, it is her family's hope that in doing so, the gift they were given in the person of Rachel Joy Scott will be a gift they can share with you. It is her family's hope that Rachel's life will make a difference to you in your own journey of faith.

—Debra K. Klingsporn

go after god.
whatever it takes, do it.....
god wants to know you now.

one

hi! i'm rachel joy scott

> Go after God. Whatever it takes, do it. And don't give the excuse, "I am just a teenager" or "I'll do that when I grow up," because it doesn't work that way. God wants to know you NOW.
>
> —Rachel Scott
>
> From a chapter titled, "What do I do about God?"
> for a book Rachel was in the process of writing

Hi. I'm Rachel Joy Scott. I love life, hate to cook, love to act, and hate being late—for anything. You may recognize my name. You may know something about me. But I want you to know *me*. The me that changed on March 5, 1993. That's the day I accepted Christ.

Before then, I was just a normal twelve-year-old. I loved sleepovers, pizza, talking on the phone, and shopping—just about in that order. Well, maybe talking on the phone should be higher on the list. But anyway, my life pretty much centered around getting a new CD or giving my brothers a hard time. Going to movies. Hanging out with my friends. Finding any excuse to laugh. You know—regular stuff.

But when I was twelve, I went to see my aunt and uncle in Shreveport, Louisiana. And they were *really* into church. Now you have to know that my family went to church, too. I had grown up going to church, but our church wasn't like *this* one. At my aunt and uncle's church, everyone acted like they had ants in their pants. They jumped around and danced and raised their hands in the air and clapped and said "Amen" out loud all the time, and let me tell you—*that* felt totally random! Well anyway, I had gone to church with my aunt and uncle before, so I knew what to expect. I just thought it was all pretty weird—not spooky or anything, just kinda strange—until *that* night.

You know how some dates just stand out in your mind? Like your best friend's birthday? (I can *always* remember my best friend's birthday, and I can *never* remember my mom's or dad's—kinda sad, huh?) Or the day you got braces? Some days you just *remember.*

Well, March 5, 1993, is one of those *remember* days for me. Even the church itself was kinda weird. Can you imagine a church with no windows? Not even stained-glass windows? Why would anyone want to build a building with no windows!?!

But I went to church with my aunt, uncle, and cousins, and right there in the middle of all these "Amens" and "Hallelujahs," right in the middle of people jumping and dancing and doing stuff I thought was so weird, something happened. I felt something inside pushing me, like an invisible hand was at my back gently getting me out of my seat and down the aisle. It was like God had snuck up on me when I was least aware that God was even in the neighborhood.

I don't think I would have been so surprised if it had happened in the mountains, like when you walk outside in the early morning light and the dew glistens and the mist hangs low. At times like that, all you need to do is *breathe* and God feels near. But in a hot, stuffy church with no windows and all that noise? There I was, in the middle of what I had always thought was so funny—till that night—and before I knew it, I was walking slowly down the aisle toward the front of the church. Everyone was at the altar and I felt so drawn, like something inside me was saying, "Go!" And so I did.

> There was no fuss or fanfare—Rachel just quietly walked down front and within moments had her hands raised and very sweetly started praying in the Spirit.
>
> —Rachel's Aunt LaBrilla

I didn't intend to do it. I didn't really *decide* to do it. I just slowly walked down the aisle till I reached the front. I sorta looked around and then closed my eyes and then raised my hands toward heaven. I don't remember what I said, but I will *never* forget the feeling. That night, I gave my life to Jesus. That night, I said yes to God.

But saying yes to God isn't like turning on a light bulb and making what was once completely dark now completely visible. Saying yes to God is more like saying yes! to an adventure—every day on the journey, you see more, ask more, learn more, and know more. And you just can never tell where God will lead you.

I remember wondering, later, exactly what *had* I done? Was I going to be weird now? Will my friends think I'm not fun anymore? Will the me on the outside be different from the me on the inside? I made the decision that night to give my life to God, but that was only the beginning. Knowing what that meant didn't happen all at once. In Shreveport, I wasn't with my friends, wasn't walking the halls of my school or hassling my brothers. The decision I made that night started a chain reaction in my life—and it was the best decision I ever made.

So if you know what it's like, or if you *want* to know what it's like to be a teen *and* a Christian—to want to live *every* moment to the fullest and feel what it means to ask God to be in the big middle of it all—then keep reading. I'll share some of my questions and doubts, my hopes and dreams, my ups and downs—and what it means to me to be a Christian, a teenager, and, well, just an ordinary girl.

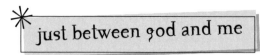

just between god and me

always,
Rachel Joy

start a
chain reaction
of love

two
just a normal girl

> **Rachel** was just a **normal girl** willing to be **used by God** to start a **chain reaction** of **love.**
>
> —Craig Scott
>
> Rachel's brother

I'm seventeen. I'm a pretty normal kid. I love my family. Have great friends. I like drama, photography, video games, and classic old movies. One of my favorites is *Arsenic and Old Lace* with Cary Grant—I've watched it a zillion times!

I have kinda short, *very* straight brown hair that's tinted red. My mom thinks I tinted it this color for a part in the school play, but I just used the play as an excuse—I really just wanted to do something funky, and tinting my hair red seemed a lot less painful and less permanent than piercing my bellybutton.

Unlike some of my friends, I like my name. Rachel Joy Scott. Clean. Simple. Only fourteen letters total; count the spaces and the period at the end and it's only seventeen characters—and that's shorter than some *last* names.

I usually sign my name *Rachel Joy*. That's because I like the word *joy*. It's one of those words that doesn't get worn out, doesn't sound corny, and when you really think about it, joy is kinda hard to define. Joy is one of those things that if you don't have it, you want it. If you do have it, something special is going on inside and words just don't do it justice. Oh yeah, that's another thing I like—words. I like to write them. I like to draw doodles around them. I like to write poetry, but not always in rhyme. And yes, I *do* get off the subject.

Back to Joy. I like having *Joy* for my middle name because I feel like my parents gave me an instruction manual for living by giving me that name—but I don't think they did it on purpose. I don't think they *knew* they were giving me my very own personalized set of instructions for living; it just sorta happened. The instructions are embedded in the letters of my name. I

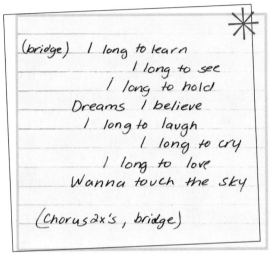

learned what this is called in English (yes, I *was* paying attention that day). It's called an acronym—that's when the letters of a word stand for something else. So, here's my very own personalized acronym, my instruction manual:

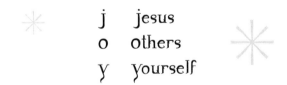

j   jesus
o   others
y   yourself

The first two are easy (well, most of the time). It's that last one that gets me in trouble. But that's what I want to tell you about—myself. I hope in telling my story you will see something of your own story in a new way. And I hope by telling my story, you will hear another story in a new way— the story of what it means to live for Christ. But first, want to play around with word doodles? This is the kind of stuff I like to do—write the initials of my name down the side of the page and think of words that make me ME (or the "me" I'd like to be)!

Kinda like this—

R   Real. Ready. Responsible (well, most of the time . . .).

A   Affectionate. Asking. AWARE.

C   Compassionate. Caring. Considerate.

H   Herself! Honest.

E   Everything! I want to experience Everything!

L   Loving. Lost. Lonely . . . sometimes.

J   Jesus. That's all. That's EVERYTHING. Jesus.

O   Others.

Y   Yourself.

Now it's your turn. Write the letters of your name down the side of the page and then write whatever words come to mind that describe *you*.

Moving right along . . .

Okay. So now you know I'm a Christian. You know God is *really* important to me. But getting back to God and me and my life, I guess if I'm going to tell you about me, the best place to start is by telling you about my family.

When it comes to family, not everybody's as lucky as me. From stuff my friends say about *their* families, I think a lot of people think their families are both a blessing and a curse—you know, can't live with 'em, can't live without 'em. And yeah, sometimes I feel that way, too. But mostly I feel lucky. Mostly I think my family is all blessing—even on the days I'm mad, aggravated, impatient, or crabby with them. 'Cause I have a great family.

Even though we have our share of hassles and problems and we get *really* annoyed at each other, we all agree on one thing—God. Everyone in my family is a Christian and I mean *everyone*. Grandparents, mom, dad, sisters, brothers, stepdad—well, everyone except the dog, and I don't know about Snuggles. But d-o-g *is* G-o-d spelled backward, and dogs *do* teach us a lot about unconditional love and forgiveness and *being there* for those we love, so if you ask me, *everyone* in my family is a Christian.

My dad was in full-time ministry, and he's a great Bible teacher, so if I ever have a question, I ask him. The thing I like about my dad is that he's willing to say, "I don't know" if he really doesn't know. But then he'll say, "Rachel, I don't know the answer to that, but I'll find out." My mom and dad both think that asking the right questions is as important as finding the right answers, but that's getting ahead of myself.

I love my parents. My mom and my stepdad, Larry, my dad and his fiancée (who is my soon-to-be-stepmom). I love them all so much. I'm one of the lucky ones because I've got parents that really care about me, and *most* of the time they're pretty cool. But sometimes . . . sometimes I just can't stand them—and I know that is *totally* natural. I hear so many teenagers who say they hate their parents. They bad-mouth them and rip them to shreds. It's such a bummer. Even when I can't stand my parents and wish they'd just leave me alone, I still try to remember that they put up with me when I'm pretty hard to live with, so I try to cut them some slack.

But even with parents that really love me, even being one of the lucky ones, sometimes I just don't get my parents. Sometimes I have a really hard time, and I feel angry and resentful.

My friend Sam told me that God had put my mom and dad in my life for a reason and God would help me figure out how to deal with how I felt. She wrote me back and said, "I know this isn't exactly what you want to hear but it's true. I know that God will totally help you with your parents, and I know deep down you love your mom and your dad. It may be a while before you realize it but just wait."

Well, I decided the best thing I could do was pray for my parents and pray for me and pray that God would show me how to *talk*

✳ June 2

Sam

~ I have so much going on inside. Yet I can't think of a single thing to say. I love my dad... but I can't go back. I don't want to. I am so pathetic... I really am. I think that everything is all good, but then I realize that... I don't know that I'm just telling myself that so that maybe someday I will truly believe it. I just want to leave. Go somewhere where nobody knows me & I could be anybody w/any kind of past. I am going to write my dad a letter telling him everything. Gotta go

L. Joy

to my parents. I asked God to help me hear my parents' side of things without getting all defensive or saying things I didn't really mean.

How did I decide that? Because I have this friend who does just that—and I admire her so much. Now she has it really rough at home. Her mom is an alcoholic and her dad is . . . well, the way my friend puts it is, her dad is "not exactly around." Every weekend my friend's mom buys alcohol for herself and her older daughter, and every weekend, my friend sees her mom and sister get plastered. A lot of teens would think this is *awesome,* like party time, here we come! But how awesome is it really to see your sister getting plastered with your mom every weekend? It's not at all pretty. In fact, from what my friend tells me, it's really ugly. And there's nothing cool about it, if you ask my friend or me.

The reason I admire this friend so much is because she's a Christian, and her faith is so strong that she refuses to join in. She doesn't rag on her mom or her sister. She doesn't tell them not to get drunk. She doesn't come across like a self-righteous, holier-than-thou jerk. All she does is pray for them . . . and I think God is going to reward her for that . . . because loving them and praying for them even while you hate what they're doing takes a lot of guts. I don't know a whole lot of people who could withstand that . . . in fact, I don't know if I could. My friend's mom messes up all the time, every weekend, but my friend says she has learned what *not* to be when she grows up.

But, back to *my* family, I kinda blew right past the part about a stepdad and a soon-to-be-stepmom. But if you caught that, you figured out that my parents are divorced. They divorced when I was seven, and yeah, it *was* a bummer. By the time their marriage started falling apart, there were five of us kids, my two older sisters, Bethanee and Dana, my two younger brothers, Craig and Michael, assorted household pets, and me in the middle. As I already told you, my dad was a minister until he and my mom divorced. Then he took what he called a "career detour." He didn't quit working for God; he just quit working for a church. But that decision meant he had to start all over trying to figure out what to do with his life—and *that* meant that there was no regular income and money was always real tight.

My dad started a new business when he took his career detour. We kids would spend the school week with my mom and weekends with my dad.

At first, he didn't even have an apartment; he lived in an office building. Every weekend we'd take our sleeping bags, roll them out on the floor, and stay at the office building with Dad. We thought it was *great* because there were big empty rooms to run around in, and my dad usually had videos, coloring books, keyboards, and games for us. But it was *really* hard on my dad—and I didn't realize how hard at the time. I just thought it was a funky place to go hang out.

Probably the most awful time for our family was when I realized things between Mom and Dad weren't going to work out, and she started working all kinds of odd jobs. My mom had always been a preacher's wife, and then suddenly, she had to figure out how to help feed five kids and pay for a house and keep the lights on and all that *grown-up* stuff. She cleaned houses and painted rooms—she did *anything* that came along. But she never made us feel like things weren't going to be okay. She said, "God's

I remember playing with office equipment and being able to photocopy our faces and hands. We could turn on microphones and speakers and try out our karaoke skills. We loved to pretend we were Whitney Houston. We played a lot of board games and were creative in how we entertained ourselves. We also did gymnastics in one of the bigger office rooms.

Our first Christmas at Dad's office, Mamaw and Papaw (dad's parents) came over. Dad tried to fix a nice meal. The only problem was, he couldn't cook more than one thing at a time, so about every fifteen minutes, a new dish was served. He didn't know how to coordinate the food so that everything was ready at once. We still tease him about his cooking skills.

—Bethanee Scott, Rachel's sister

never let us go hungry, and we've always had a roof over our heads. God will take care of this, too."

Like one time we had this old, clunker car and the tires were so bald you could have almost used them for giant rubber bands. Well, my mom was worried about driving us around on Colorado streets in the winter with slick tires.

My mom is this little-bitty, polite, petite, pretty woman that you think is quiet and nice and won't want to make waves. And she *is* soft-spoken and sweet—until it comes to someone messing with her family. Then she's this little *fireball*.

Like one day after school, my two brothers had been down the street playing at a neighbor's house. My mom got home from work, went into the kitchen, and started frying chicken. All of a sudden, Mike and Craig came running into the house, totally out of breath, looking scared and panicky, when seconds later a woman none of us knew came storming into our house. Before I knew it, this woman was standing in our living room, yelling at my mom. She said the boys had thrown a rock at her car, and she had followed them home. This lady was *really* mad and just stood there, yelling at my mom, yelling at my brothers. We were all freaking out.

Well, my mom wasn't going to have some strange lady standing in her house yelling at her kids. She told the lady that she would deal with my brothers and showed her the door. But that wasn't good enough. About fifteen minutes later a policeman showed up, but by that time my mom had already scolded my brothers, given them both spankings, and gone back to frying chicken.

So anyway, this police officer started to question my mom. But she just cut him short.

"Now, Officer, that lady really wanted to start a fight and I was not going to stand here in my house and argue with her," my mom said. "I have already disciplined my boys, just as I told that lady I would, but I did *not* spank my boys for the sake of pleasing that woman. I did it because they needed to be corrected and it was the right thing to do for my sons."

Well, that police officer didn't have too much to say after that. He thanked my mom *very* politely and left like he was tiptoeing on broken glass—and we never heard another word from the police *or* that woman. But the really funny thing is, the rock didn't hit the car, and after the policeman left, my mom just went back to frying chicken and we had supper a little later than usual that night. Doesn't matter if it's a lady yelling at her or a policeman asking questions, when it comes to my brothers, sisters, and me, my mom knows her mind and nothing can stop her.

Well, anyway, back to our old car and those bald tires. My mom would walk around the house praying out loud about those silly tires, telling God she needed new tires for her kids to be safe when she was driving us to school and doctor's appointments. She'd say, "God, I don't know how I'm going to pay for new tires. I know you know what we need, but are you aware, God, that there's absolutely no tread on those tires?"

In one of the Gospels Jesus tells a story about a woman who absolutely *hounded* God with prayer. She wouldn't leave God alone, just prayed and prayed and prayed. My dad says that story isn't about us changing God's mind. It's about how prayer changes us. He says that when we keep praying for the same thing over and over, things become clearer in our own thinking—and in time we see the difference between what we *want* and what we really *need*. Well, my mom prayed so much she was constantly in God's face—like that woman in the parable—and there was *no* doubt in her mind that those tires were "need-ers," not "want-ers."

So she went to work one day. That morning she'd been doing her usual in-God's-face kind of praying about those tires . . . winter was coming . . . Colorado roads . . . ice and snow. . . . She drove to work—and there, sitting in the driveway of the place she worked were four brand-new tires out with the garbage!

Even my mom couldn't believe it at first. She went inside, asked her boss if those tires were sitting out with the garbage by mistake, and nope, the owner was throwing them out. So my mom had been going around the house, praying while she was doing the dishes and muttering like a madwoman, telling God how worried she was about driving five kids all over everywhere in an old car with bald tires—and then boom! There are four tires sitting out with the garbage that just *happened* to be the exact size we needed for our car. Those tires may have been somebody else's garbage, but they were *my* mom's miracle. I don't have a clue why someone would throw away four brand-new tires, but my mom says it's all part of God's economy.

I know that not everyone has a mom who goes around the house praying and muttering about tires and lunch money and a leaky roof and who knows what else. But with a mom like that and a dad who sees a lesson in just about everything—you have to admit—I was kinda set up to take this God stuff seriously. And I do, not always and not every day, but God just seems to have a special hold on my life.

So back when my parents and I were going through some hard times and I found myself feeling angry and not wanting to be around much, I learned a lot from my friend. After my parents split and we were trying to live in two homes, when it seemed like everyone was mad at everyone else all the time, when all I wanted to do was escape to my room or yell at my brothers, I learned a lot from my friend. I started praying for my family, just like my friend prayed for her mom and sister. I prayed a lot.

And you know what? Praying helped. Having two families got to be *really* okay and getting better—because asking God to be in the big middle of everything makes a big difference. Not all at once. But gradually. Little by little. Praying like that woman in the parables, praying like my mom does, is kind of like trying to grow your hair out or taking vitamins or getting over a cold—changes from day to day don't seem like a big deal. But if you keep paying

---

> January 21st, 98
>
> Dear God,
>
> I ask for your help in this household. I ask that you replace the hate, with your love. I ask that you soften hearts, open eyes, and silence tongues. I ask that we come together not just as a family, but a family in Christ. I thank you for each member and I thank you for each blessing that will come upon them. I rebuke Satan in the name of Jesus. I bind him from this family
>
> Amen

attention, before you know it, you wake up one day and wow! Things are different. Things are cool.

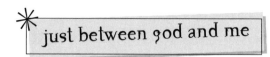

just between god and me

So. What do you wish was different in your life? What's tough in your family? What kind of "tires" do *you* need? (Okay, think metaphorically.) Are you willing to pray about it and give God a chance? Just remember, there's no right or wrong here. There's no bad prayer. You just tell God how you feel and what you wish. Go ahead. Give it a try. Just start off by writing, *Dear God, I'm here . . .* and see where your thoughts go next, because wherever your thoughts go, God's right there, too.

-Proverbs 3

Pos: 3:3 "Let love & faithfulness never leave you;
    bind them around your neck;
    write them on the tablet of your
    heart."

↗everyone?
    3:5,6 "Trust in the Lord with all your heart
    and & lean not on your own understanding
    in all your ways acknowledge him,
    and he will make your paths straight."

the Lord
disciplines
those he
loves

✳DO NOT BE WISE IN YOUR OWN EYES;
FEAR THE LORD AND SHUN ᵗⁿᵉᵍˡᵉᶜᵗ EVIL" PDS 3:7

"DO NOTS"... PDS 3:27-32

3:31
DO NOT ENVY
A VIOLENT MAN
OR CHOOSE ANY OF HIS
WAYS. ᵉᵛⁱ?

What is life when living without the Lifemaker?

acknowledging him
is not having a
relationship with him

three

not perfect—just forgiven

Before I go off on what you **should** and **should not** do . . . I'll start with what I did. I grew up **knowing** that **God exists**. A lot of people think that this is enough. **IT'S NOT**. Acknowledging him is not having a relationship with him.

—Rachel Scott

From a chapter titled, "What do I do about God?" for a book Rachel was in the process of writing

Okay. New Topic. What nobody *ever* talks about (or at least nobody ever told me) is that after saying yes to God, everything doesn't all of a sudden become "happily ever after." I came home a few days after that night in Louisiana and guess what? My mom and dad were still my mom and dad—and still divorced. My brothers and sisters were still my brothers and sisters, meaning of course, that my oldest sister still thought she knew everything and my little brother was still always late and all of us still got on one another's nerves. School was still school. And friends, well, in junior high, friends are *always* a good news, bad news kind of deal.

Everyone always thinks that once you accept Jesus into your heart, everything will be smooth sailing after that. You hardly ever hear about the next day and the next and the next. At least I didn't. Well, let me tell you, everything does *not* get easy after that, and happily ever after happens only in fairy tales. Accepting Jesus into my heart made a big difference for me, but it did not make everything easier. Not for me, anyway.

For me, being a Christian is hard sometimes, and I believe it's *especially* hard while you're a teen because if you take that "What Would Jesus Do?" question seriously, being a Christian means you have to do the hard thing. Like being honest, or forgiving, or kind, or choosing *not* to do some of the things your friends are doing. At least that's the way it's been for me.

Like, one of my absolute *best* friends is named Sam. Well, her name is really Samantha, but I call her Sam. She's been one of my best buds *forever.* We tell each other just about *everything*—and even keep a journal together. Actually, I keep a journal with God, a journal with Sam, and most of the time I've got journals going with other friends, too.

> april 12, 98
>
> Dear Sam,
>
> Well, I have a diary with Jeff, a diary with God, and now a diary with you. This will be for our eyes only. We can pass it off Mondays, Wednesdays, and any other time we see each other. This book has no limitations. You can write letters, thoughts, poems, feelings, songs... anything. Write now, I'm going to share my first poem with you. I wrote this in 6th grade at camp, and even though its my first, I think its my best.

As I was weeping & crying,
I fell to my knee,
I heard the Lord's voice,
He was speaking to me,
He said there would be,
No more sins, no more lies
Only peace & happiness,
In all of my cries.

It's not my best because
It rhymes and its catchy.
It's not deep, it's not
complicated, it's not
much. It's beautiful to me
because it was written
with faith like a child.
That faith was so simple
and easy to understand. But
with age comes complexity.
Now, I seek that same faith
and would give anything to
have it back.

Always,
Rachel Joy

Anyway, Sam and I both want to be actresses. We both get into school plays in a big way. We both love to act. You get the picture.

Not only do I *want* to be an actress, but I've *always* wanted to be an actress. Before I could tie my shoelaces, I began thinking of my acceptance speech for the Academy Awards! My dad would laugh and think I was kidding when I'd say, "Someday, Dad, you're going to see me on *Oprah!*" Well, I wasn't kidding. I just *knew* I was going to be famous!

So, I started my first year in high school, auditions for the school play were coming up, I had my eye on the lead—and then I found out my *best friend* had the lead part! Sam got the part before I even knew what was happening. I was so bummed! I kept thinking God had gotten things mixed up. I was disappointed, ticked off, hurt . . . but more than that—I was jealous! I wanted to be mad at somebody or something. I wanted to scream and throw a temper tantrum like a little kid in a grocery store who can't have the Oreos *now.* Know what I mean?

Well, if you're *not* a Christian, none of that's a problem. Well, you probably wouldn't throw a temper tantrum in a store if you're old enough to worry about acne, but you can be mad. You can be jealous. You can be ticked off at your best friend for no good reason—and you don't have to answer to anybody. But if you're a Christian, you've got to answer to God, right? All that stuff I hear about in church sounds different when I take it to school.

✳ ✳ ✳

Like most young Christians, Rachel for the most part enjoyed keeping her prayer life in a private, personal, intimate kind of way. But there were many times at church and youth service where I saw her praying aloud with her other Christian friends. Sometimes they would pray in small circles while holding hands and other times, it was laying hands on individuals and lifting them up in prayer.

She prayed many times on her knees, hands on her face, head down. It was like she was imagining the world had disappeared and it was just her and God, and they were sharing their hearts, and she would tell him all her secrets, and he would listen and whisper in her ear how much he loved her, often bringing tears to her eyes.

Rachel liked to pray in her room while listening to her favorite Christian songs, usually turning up the music loud enough to drown out her own voice. I saw her do this several times. I remember a few times when she and I prayed aloud together on our way to youth group in the car. It was almost always prayer concerning our own family. Some of her thankful prayers were very often boldly expressed at youth group and church. Jumping up and down when excited—raising her arms to God—was not uncommon for Rachel. Sometimes she would find her own little corner while other times, she would stand right at the front of the stage.

—Dana Scott, Rachel's sister

✳　✳　✳

My mom says that if doing the right thing were easy, then it wouldn't be such a big deal because everybody would do the right thing. If being a Christian were *easy*, everyone would do it, not because they wanted to know God, but because they wanted to have an easy life, right?

Well, I knew I couldn't stay upset. I knew I had to talk to God about the way I felt about Sam getting the lead. I knew I had to work on my attitude. So, I prayed when I was going to school. I

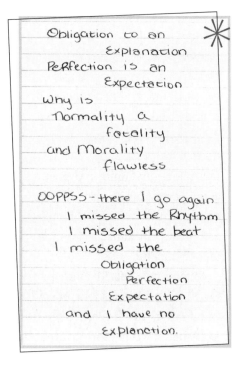

Obligation to an
Explanation
PeRfection is an
Expectation
Why is
normality a
fatality
and morality
flawless

OOPPSS - there I go again
I missed the Rhythm
I missed the beat
I missed the
Obligation
Perfection
Expectation
and I have no
Explanation.

-What kinda life is this?
Life handed her the face—
    made her the model

-What kinda life is this?
Life handed her the athletics—
    made her the sportshero e.

-What kinda life is this?
Life handed her the curves
    Made her the pin up girl.

LIFE gave her
        the face, the athletics, the curves
life left me with
    personality, deep thoughts,
        and self respect

And in this society, in this life—
Most would say that
    I have been cheated
Out of what's important.

I am woman
on rather, on the verge
of womanhood

You are man
the opposite of what
I represent.

We are beings
The same yet different
Our souls know no sex
They are spiritual
beautiful, precious

So why
if we posess
the same, both
which are the most
important existances
we have
why
do I getted treated as the
lower sex

prayed when I was sitting on my bed, trying (not too successfully) to concentrate on homework. I told God how lousy I felt, how disappointed I was. I wrote poems, not just about my feelings about my family, but poems about everything, and let the words in the poems be honest, completely bummed, questioning, or hopeful.

But once I started talking to God, being honest about what I was feeling, my feelings started to change. I wrote in my journal.

I tried to be honest with God and with myself. And then, I let God do the rest—I let God change my attitude and give me a different feeling about everything. And God is awesome.

3/2/98

Dear God,

I know that at first I was really jealouse of Sam. She's sweet, pretty, popular, & she got the major part for the drama. But now I only admire those qualities. You have blessed her with gifts & talents and I can only be happy for her. Thank you for giving her lead role in the drama. It has taught me that I won't always be in the spot light. I am thankful to have a chance to be in the drama at all. Tommorrow I have an audition. I am not expecting to get a part. If I don't, I promise not to critize or become jealous of those who make it. If I get a part, I promise not to let it go to my head, and I will remember to thank Thee, for the ability, strength, courage, & talent you blessed me with. I don't want to be successful without you God. I can't be successful without you.

Love always,
Rachel Joy

Even in ordinary stuff—like being jealous of a friend, or getting embarrassed because a teacher yelled at me instead of the other kid who was talking in class and not paying attention, or feeling resentful that my sister got some new clothes and I didn't—walking with God is hard sometimes. Because God doesn't cut us any slack. When God says to forgive, God means to forgive no matter what. When God says to be honest, that means no white lies. When God says we are supposed to love one another, that means even people we may not particularly *like*. And if at times it's hard, maybe being hard is the only way God knows that we're choosing to love God—no matter what. Understand what I'm saying? I hate it when people explain things over and over like you don't know what they are getting at, so I don't want to go on and on.

But, my life as a Christian is hard sometimes. Making the right choices is hard sometimes. Taking the time to pray is hard sometimes. Knowing what's right and what's wrong is hard sometimes. And, well, I wanted you to know that it could be that way for you, too, but following God is worth it—no matter how hard it can be.

But if it's hard sometimes, how do I get through the hard part? What does it mean to follow God?

To me, it means (first of all), having a *relationship* with God. Just like you would with your best friend. But what does *that* mean, like how do you get a relationship with someone you can't see, hear, or touch?

I'll start by telling you what I did. As you already know, I grew up knowing God exists. A lot of people think that's enough. Trust me, IT'S NOT. Acknowledging God is *not* the same as having a relationship. So many people don't realize that you can talk to God just as you talk to anyone else. You can make God smile. You can make God laugh. You can make God cry. To have a relationship with God, all you have to do is talk to him.

I started learning how to talk to God by writing how I felt. I'd sit on my bed in my room, close the door, and start doodling. I guess in some ways I started taking God seriously sooner than some of my friends. But I just *needed* to: my mom and dad had their hands full working and being single parents; my two older sisters are close to the same age and had each other; my two younger brothers are only a year apart, and they had each other. I was stuck in the middle and a lot of times just felt like the Lone Ranger.

I think I started writing stuff down about how I felt and what I thought in, well, maybe sixth grade, at least that's as early as I can remember. Most of what I can find in the clutter and chaos of my room (which my mom usually describes as a disaster zone, but hey, I like it) are pages of scribbles that sound pretty silly now. But I think that words written down on a page kinda take on a life of their own.

Sometimes I think about Anne Frank writing in her journal in a stuffy, closed up, dark attic in Amsterdam during World War II. She was just being a normal kid, wishing she could be out shopping and noticing cute guys instead of being stuck for two years in that un-fun, cramped, and crowded hiding place. She wrote about being lonely. About butting heads with her mom. About who was mean to who and what hunger felt like and how *frustrating* it was to not go outside. She confided and whined and complained and questioned. She even wrote, "In bed at night, as I ponder my many sins and exaggerated shortcomings, I get so confused by the sheer amount . . . that I either laugh or cry, depending on my mood. Then I fall asleep with the strange feeling of wanting to be different than I am . . ."

And look at what became of her journals. Wow. Talk about a life of their own!

When words are put on a page, you never know what might happen. So I kept my sixth-grade notebooks, just because I'm too much of a pack rat to throw them out. And I do think it's pretty funny to look at what my handwriting looked like then (I'm so glad *that* has changed with time!).

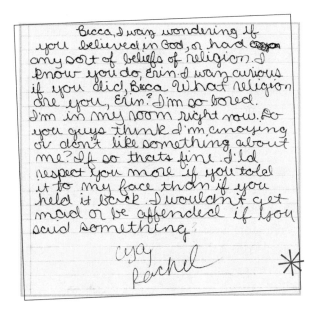

But probably the most important thing about looking at what I wrote when I was younger is realizing that the way I felt then was the way most everyone felt. I wasn't weird, even though I felt that way sometimes. So if that was true then, it's probably still true. Sometimes I'd even stop myself and tell myself to just stop *thinking* that way. I just have a hard time remembering that on days I feel ugly, weird, unpopular, confused, bummed out, or just plain tired and crabby.

But *everyone* has those days. Being a Christian doesn't make that go away. Being a Christian just gives me a different way of dealing with terrible, lousy, rotten, no-good, very bad days. When I feel lousy, I tell God. When I feel confused, I tell God. When I feel hurt, betrayed, depressed, lonely—any of that bad stuff—I tell God. I write it out.

In the Bible, when the Hebrews wanted to have God bless something, they would bring it to the temple and lay it down at the altar. That was their way of giving something to God. Well, when I write stuff down, my journal kinda becomes my altar—I write it all out, tell God or a friend how lousy I feel, and then leave it there on the page. I can't explain it. Don't know why it works. Don't know how it works. But I just know that after I do that, I feel better. Even if the next day I feel just as bad and have to do it all over again.

Eternity Now

Breakthrough Retreat   3-7-98
   God... I have this terrible sharp, dull pain in my stomach. I don't know if it's a spiritual feeling, if the enemy is attacking, or if it's just sickness what-ever it is, I just ask for your healing. If it's a spiritual feeling, I ask you to bless it. If it's the enemy, I ask you to bind it. If it's just sickness I ask you to heal it. Thank you

   Rachel Joy

I stand back, God, and I watch those around me and ask myself, What is it that they're feeling? What is it that they're thinking? Are they seeing you? Can they hear you? If so, why can't I? What am I doing so wrong that I can't reach that level? Everyone looks at me and thinks, wow, what a together kinda girl. She's doing good. But you know God that I'm not. Why won't you fix that? I don't understand. This feeling is killing me, God. Why don't you do something? I know that you have already done so much, but why stop there? I want to reach a new level with you God. Take me there. Please, God, take me there. I want that so much. I want to serve you. I want to be used by you to help others. But I feel like I can't do that until you change this feeling I have. Come to me God, and make use of me.

Your servant,
Rachel Joy

✳

When I was little I used to love those little magic pen scratching sets. You know what I mean—those doodling deals where you use a pointed plastic writing thing to draw on a gray plastic sheet; then when you're done, you lift the plastic cover and the image disappears and you can start all over again. Well, I think telling God what I feel by writing it down on paper is kinda like that.

I write it down and even though the words stay on the paper, God somehow lifts the ugly feelings inside me. I feel better, like the day is a new day, or I've got an idea about how to resolve a problem, or I find the energy to do something I couldn't do before.

When I read back through my journals, I sometimes think, *Man! I was really bummed out,* but I don't usually go back and take the time to write about my gratitude or excitement or relief. But that's okay, too, because the guys who wrote the Psalms did the same thing. They would plead and complain and whine and question and even argue with God.

My dad says that some people are uncomfortable with that kind of honesty; he says the people who say Christians should have faith instead of honestly admitting they struggle with feelings like anger, doubt, resentment, and fear are just scared. I see his point. If God didn't want us to be honest about how we feel, then why would so many of the Psalms have phrases like "How long, O LORD? Will you forget me forever? How long will you hide your face from me?" (Ps. 13:1). I mean, you can't get much more honest than *that!*

So, I stand by what I've written. Even if some of the poems don't rhyme as well as I wish. Even if some of the prayers are as bleak as a Colorado moonscape above the timberline. Even if someone reads what I wrote and thinks, *Whoa! Was this kid depressed or what!?!* I know that God is faithful. I know that God sees me through even my toughest days. I

> Rachel and I had a number of talks about honesty. I remember specifically telling her that many people are afraid to be brutally honest with God. I encouraged her that that kind of honesty was what God wanted from us.
>
> —Darrell Scott,
> Rachel's father

know that God brought my family back together even though my parents are still divorced. And I know that God is present even when everything feels so dark that I think the sun will never shine. So, no matter what I feel, I keep putting words on paper. I keep telling God about . . . whatever.

Well, when it comes to having a relationship with God, I could sit here and tell you what to do and what to say and how to pray, but where will that get you if you just sit there? So I'm not going to go off on what you should and should not do. Best thing I can tell you is, go after God. Trust me . . . well, better yet . . . trust God. Christianity is not a label, but a lifestyle, something that has to be lived from the inside out. I hope you let God in. I hope you start talking to God—doesn't matter what about. And hey, if there's anything I know that I wish you knew, it's this: God is present in the darkness even when it doesn't feel that way.

just between god and me

How about you? What do you believe? Go ahead. Give it a try. Make a list. Do some verbal doodles. (And while you're at it, take a look at Psalm 139 or Isaiah 43:1.)

i believe—

. . . .

. . . .

. . . .

. . . .

. . . .

. . . .

. . . .

. . . .

Father, reach out Your hand,
Grab a hold of my life.
Open my eyes,
To Your wonderful light.
Fill me up,
With Your undying love.
Save me a place,
In Your kingdom above.

~ by Rachel Joy Scott

I wrote this song, and when I wrote it, it was intended to motivate Christians to go preach the Gospel to the world. But by the time I got to the second verse, I realized that I should be talking to myself instead of everyone else. I should be taking my own advice. And as Christians, we need to remember to walk our talk.

always!!!

take a risk,
chance it,
trust
in god

don't give up

> "I had my ups and downs and I fell a few times, but I did not give up. Don't give up, because God's reward is worth it all. . . . I challenge you to listen, and see what God will do. Take a risk, chance it, trust in God. . . . You will see what God can do with a willing heart."
>
> —Rachel Scott
>
> From a chapter titled, "What do I do about God?"
> for a book Rachel was in the process of writing

My mom has this thing about maturity. When I was sixteen, almost seventeen, I *still* didn't have my driver's license, much less a car. My mom wouldn't let me take the driver's license test because she thought I wasn't mature enough.

I'd ask her when I could get my license. I'd "remind" my mom that everyone else got to take the driver's license test the day they turned sixteen, but my mom would say, "Just because it's the law doesn't mean it's the law *here*."

Talk about a bummer! I *hate* it when my mom gets that *look*. Know what I mean? That determined, nonnegotiable, "my mind is made up!" kind of look. I know when I see that "Rachel, don't mess with me" kind of look that I might as well give it up—there's no use pressing it. She's like the iron lady.

Anyway, my mom has this thing about maturity. She said it wasn't me she didn't trust; it's what all the other people out there might choose to do. That didn't make a whole lot of sense to me, but after making me think I'd probably be close to twenty-one before she'd let me drive, she *finally* let me get my driver's license *because* she trusts me.

But she didn't always. I used to get into trouble. You know, break my curfew or not call and tell her where I was if I went home with a friend, "forget" to do my homework and get bad grades. I wasn't messing up big time with drugs or anything like that. I just wasn't being "responsible" or acting very respectful toward my parents. I blew off doing chores around the house and didn't take school very seriously.

On the outside, everybody thought I was this great Christian kid, you know, upbeat, funny, smart. But on the inside, I felt awkward and ugly. Didn't matter what others told me. Couldn't believe the compliments. I felt like no matter what I did, it wasn't good enough. I didn't feel that way every day. Just some days, but, well, enough days that I had to go to summer school after eighth grade. I just had a hard time in eighth grade, but you know what? Since I've been in high school, I've talked to a lot of girls who had a hard time in junior high.

> When Mom was in eighth grade, her family moved from a small town to a much larger city. Mom had always been a good student, but this move caused her to go into a bad slump. Her grades dropped, and she felt so displaced with no friends. She told me that this was such a hard year and a half, and it wasn't until she was in tenth grade that she was able to pull herself together. During all of this time, however, she was pretending to be okay with others, herself, and especially God.
>
> Mom told me that it was normal and okay to have those feelings. She said that it was all a part of growing up. Almost everyone experiences insecurities, especially in junior high.
>
> —Rachel Joy Scott

Maybe it's because in junior high everything changes so fast, but then again, some things don't change fast enough. I remember feeling like everything in my life was changing and sometimes I wasn't sure I *liked* the changes. I was too big for my dad to pick me up, throw me over his shoulder and spin around, but I wasn't big *enough* to go to the mall with my friends without one of my big sisters coming along. I was *too* big to play on jungle gyms or playgrounds, but *not* big enough to see movies with PG-13 ratings—even though all my friends could.

Sometimes I felt like there were two of me. The "outside" me that everybody could see and thought was upbeat, funny, and smart. And the "inside" me—the me that only God and I knew. I think I understand why Adam and Eve wanted to run and hide from God when they were in the Garden of Eden. Sometimes I wished I could, too. Only the one I wanted to hide from was *me*.

* * *

I could see this time in Rachel's life as probably the hardest. She was really beginning to question things about life in general and trying to think things through for herself. I think her deep questions about God started to come during this time. The divorce probably seemed the most real that it had ever felt because she was beginning to really see what was going on, and she was observing how it was affecting the family, like Bethanee and me.

Rachel went to a Christian school in the sixth and seventh grades, and then she went back to public school in eighth. I could see how in sixth and seventh, she really began having deep thoughts about her own life and also God, because God was a subject that was in her face daily. She probably felt like her life was real bland and unexciting because our Christian school was very strict as well as small. Rachel was—being an outgoing social butterfly—probably anxious for a chance to be involved in a fast-paced school like Columbine, where she could mix with all kinds of people and spread her wings.

—Dana Scott, Rachel's sister

* * *

I think when I was in junior high I went through this massive pity party. I just didn't like my life. I felt like my family wasn't normal (whatever *normal* is! My sister Dana says *normal* is one of the most stupid words in the English language). I was upset and confused about my parents' divorce. I was bummed that my parents weren't going to get back together (doesn't everyone wish that if your parents are divorced?!?).

Well, in the middle of all that, I just got mad. Not mad at anything in particular, just mad at everything. Mad at my brothers and sisters for breathing :). Mad at my mom for being . . . well, my mom. Mad at school for being boring. It wasn't like I ran around throwing things in the house or yelling at my brothers or cussing at people for no good reason. I just felt like inside things were out of whack. I wasn't happy. I didn't keep up with my homework. I just didn't care. Know what I mean? Like the person living on the inside of my skin was having a tug-of-war with the one living on the outside.

But even when church was boring and seemed so totally irrelevant to my life, I did pay attention some of the time. Like the Sunday our preacher talked about a verse from Romans that really got my attention. Our preacher was quoting Paul, you know, the guy who wrote like half the New Testament? Mr. Super Christian? Anyway, Paul wrote in Romans, "I do not understand my own actions. For I do not do what I want, but I do the very thing I hate. . . . For I know that nothing good dwells within me . . . I can will what is right, but I cannot do it. For I do not do the good I want, but the evil I do not want is what I do."

Well, after hearing that, I went home and read that whole chapter in Romans and the one after that—Romans 7 and 8. And you know? I realized I was *normal!* Okay, yeah, I know—it's that word my sister says is stupid, but I realized *everybody* feels like they have two different people inside—the one who wants to do the right thing and the one who doesn't. Well, somehow writing about how I felt in my journal and realizing that even super-Christians like the apostle Paul struggle with emotions and actions that seem to pull in opposite directions, I don't know, it just seemed like God was working from the inside out again.

After going to summer school before I started ninth grade, I cleaned up my act. I started making good grades, and I hardly ever got into trouble.

When I started "taking responsibility" (that's what my mom calls it), my parents started trusting me more and more. They quit asking a million questions when I went out. Most of the time, they don't say no to me anymore. I have a whole lot more freedom. Once I showed them that there wasn't any reason they couldn't trust me, they let me do a whole lot more. Knowing my parents trust me to keep up with my homework, to do what I say I'll do, to come home when I say I'll be home, all that "taking responsibility" stuff, well, once I had more freedom, I didn't want to blow it.

My mom says I showed her my maturity by doing my chores without having to be reminded, taking care of my own clothes, helping around the house, working at keeping my grades up. But what really happened is that I decided it was my parents' job to do *their* best and my job to do *my* best, and since I was still the kid, it probably wasn't *my* job to decide what was best for them (like maybe it *wasn't* best for them to get back together). And maybe it was best for me to just take care of what I could take care of—like getting my homework done. Does that make any sense?

My friend with the bad family situation isn't allowed to go to church. Her mom won't let her. One time we had the opportunity for her to sneak out so she could go to church with us, but my friend said no. Even though she wanted nothing more than to go to church, she refused to go behind her mom's back. She refused to disobey her mom, even to go to *church*! And she was right. Even though her mom is wrong for not letting her go, my friend would have been just as wrong for going behind her back. As far as God's concerned, I don't think there's any excuses, well, within reason. Now if my friend's mom asked her to rob a bank . . . okay, that might be different, but I think you get where I'm going.

One of the Ten Commandments says to "honor thy father and mother." If God didn't think obeying our parents was important, I don't think God would've put it in with the other nine—so I figure it must be important. So now when my parents say I can't go out, I don't go. No big deal. I just let it go and figure it'll all work out. If you decide to start going along with your parents, and not whining, or complaining, or making a big deal when they say no, then watch their reaction. Don't ask me why, but it works. When I stopped hassling my parents, they started saying yes a lot more often. It's hard sometimes, but I've been a lot happier since I stopped being mad at my life, started showing more respect toward my mom and dad, and tried to "be responsible" . . . and my parents have, too.

A wonderful thing
Oh Power Divine,
To thank thee,
For these gifts of thine,
For summer's sunshine,
And winter's snow,
For hearts that kindle,
And thoughts that glow.

I'll be yours,
Through thick and thin,
You'll be mine,
Outside and in,
You'll always be there,
This I know,
And in my heart,
Is where you shall go.

When I feel,
Your powerful presence,
I fall to my knees,
And cry in repentance,
All I feel,
Is your wonderful love,
And this only comes,
From Heaven above.

just between god and me

So, what are the issues that you feel like your parents hassle you about? Cleaning your room? Grades? Friends? Take a minute and write some of the ways you feel hassled or think your parents are unreasonable.

Now flip it around. Why do you think your parents feel or do what they do? Are they afraid for your safety? Is it a "respect" thing? What would it look like from their side of the fence?

So, what might "honor your father and mother" look like in the middle of your hassles?

don't let your
character change
color with your
environment

find out who you are

Don't let your **character** change color with your environment. Find out **who you are** and let it stay its **true** color.

—Rachel Scott

In an undated letter to her cousin

Cute. Bubbly. Perky. Outgoing.

That's what grownups always say about me. I *hate* those words. Well, not really, but what I *want* people to say about me is . . .

"Oh, Rachel Scott? Isn't she *gorgeous?*"

Or how about "beautiful!" or "stunning"? Yeah. "Stunning." I could go for stunning! But, no. It's always "cute," "adorable," or "perky."

If I ever entered a Miss America contest, I'm sure I'd be a contender for Miss Congeniality and not stand a chance for the crown. Well, actually, I know a few girls who wouldn't give me their Miss Congeniality vote.

I had a group of girlfriends. Longtime friends. At the time I wouldn't have described us as a clique—because I *hate* cliques. I'm not into being labeled in *any* way. I don't like wearing jeans that have somebody's name on my back pocket. Forget khakis and shirts with little emblems and sweatshirts with big fat names across the front. (Like, haven't you ever wondered why Abercrombie & Fitch is a *clothes* store, but they advertise using models who don't look like they're even *wearing* clothes? The guys on the big signs in the store windows aren't even wearing shirts—and it's a store with racks and racks of shirts! Go figure! Is that not like so stupid?!)

But back to labels and friends and cliques. Looking back, I think my group of friends and I probably were pretty cliquish, because I'm kind of into definitions and when I check out what *Webster's Dictionary* says, it pretty well says it all:

clique \ klick \ *n* [f] : a narrow exclusive circle or group of persons; *esp* : one held together by a presumed identity of interest, views, or purposes.

Yup, guilty as charged. We didn't make other girls feel welcomed. We spent most of our time making fun of kids we didn't hang out with.

But like I said, at the time, I wouldn't have said *we* were a clique, because I don't know *anyone* who says *their* friends are a clique. Nobody *says* they like cliques. It's like jealousy or envy—nobody wants to *admit* they're jealous or envious, even though everyone feels jealous or envious at some time or other. Same with cliques.

If you're in a clique, you're on the inside and that's not on the side that hurts. It's only when you're on the *outside* that you see a clique for what it really is.

I know—because I've been there.

I've been on both sides, the inside *and* the outside.

I had a group of friends, and we'd been friends since grade school. We did slumber parties and had crushes and told secrets and asked each other when we were going to start wearing deodorant and told each other when we got our first bras and when we started our periods. You know. All that girl stuff. We even talked about being bridesmaids at each other's weddings! (How's that for corny?) But I believed it. I thought we'd help plan each other's high school graduation open houses and go on double dates and be roommates at college. I thought we'd be forever friends.

But when I was in ninth grade I started going to the coolest church with a youth group called Breakthrough. I went with my sister Dana because she kept bugging me about it, saying, "Rachel, this is *so* cool. You *gotta* check it out. You just gotta come with me."

Well, she bugged me so much that I finally said, "Okay, I'll go!" just to shut her up. But, you know what? She was right. It *was* cool.

Once I started going to Breakthrough, I really started to grow spiritually. I wanted to seek God with my whole heart. I wanted to love God with a passion. I didn't know a whole lot of people at that church, so for me, it was a fresh start, a group of friends who didn't know where I'd come from but did know where I was going. And I started really listening in church— not just in Wednesday night youth group, but also in Sunday morning adult church—and *that* was a big change, believe me! Before that, I'd sit in church thinking, *This is soooo B-O-R-I-N-G,* wishing I'd brought my Walkman, or wanting to write notes or sneak out.

But Breakthrough changed all that. I realized that just because someone goes to church doesn't mean that person's a Christian. And just claiming to be a Christian isn't enough. You know Christians by their lifestyle. You know them by their words and actions. You know them by what they say and do. *Christian* means being like Christ. Being like Christ does *not* mean that you just say and do good things; it means you know God—and you want to know God more.

Once all that started to really sink in, I wanted to know God like I'd never wanted to before. Knowing God became more important to me than almost anything. I started thinking about God a lot, like almost all the time. (Okay, *boys* and God . . . mmmm . . . well, that's not quite true. Not "boys" as in boys, plural, but "boys" as in a *particular* boy. . . .)

> What is faith when you are a fan instead of a follower? What is Christianity when it is a label instead of a lifestyle? What is life when living without the LIFEMAKER?
>
> I will never turn into a "social plastic friend." It's not just the end or where we begin, it is in the in-betweens.
>
> —from notes to Mark Bodiford from Rachel Scott

Our youth minister called wanting to take God more seriously beginning to "walk the talk." Well, I wanted to walk the talk. Know what I mean? I wanted to be the same girl at school that I was at youth group. I wanted people to see Jesus when they saw me. I wanted to turn heads for Christ. I wanted to be a high-impact, make-a-difference, love-the-world-and-turn-the-tide kind of Christian. Not a wimpy, polite, no big deal, politically-correct-and-don't-make-waves kind of Christian.

Well, when I started taking God more seriously, these friends, friends that I thought were forever friends, started to make fun of me. They wouldn't talk to me in the hall between classes. If I walked up to them at their lockers, they turned their backs toward me. I'd hear them giggling when I walked by. It was so awful! I didn't have any friends to sit with in the lunchroom. It was like one day we were friends, and the next day I'd been voted out, terminated, persona non grata.

I was hurt. Confused. Angry. Embarrassed.

A grown-up friend of mine who is kinda like a spiritual mentor told me

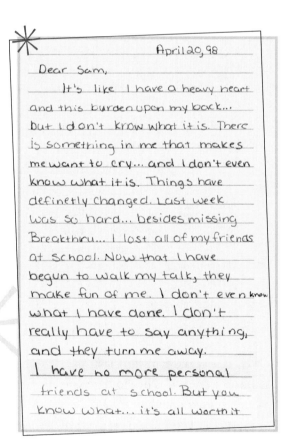

> April 20, 98
>
> Dear Sam,
>
>   It's like I have a heavy heart and this burden upon my back... but I don't know what it is. There is something in me that makes me want to cry... and I don't even know what it is. Things have definetly changed. Last week was so hard... besides missing Breakthru... I lost all of my friends at school. Now that I have begun to walk my talk, they make fun of me. I don't even know what I have done. I don't really have to say anything, and they turn me away.
>
>   I have no more personal friends at school. But you know what... it's all worth it

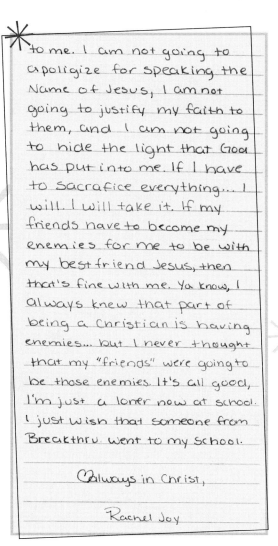

to me. I am not going to apoligize for speaking the Name of Jesus, I am not going to justify my faith to them, and I am not going to hide the light that God has put into me. If I have to sacrafice everything... I will. I will take it. If my friends have to become my enemies for me to be with my best friend Jesus, then that's fine with me. Ya know, I always knew that part of being a Christian is having enemies... but I never thought that my "friends" were going to be those enemies. It's all good, I'm just a loner now at school. I just wish that someone from Breakthru went to my school.

Always in Christ,

Rachel Joy

something really cool. She told me about this group of Christians a long time ago who had funny ways of saying stuff. They were called Quakers (yeah, like in Quaker Oats . . .). Anyway, Quakers talked about God working in their lives by "way opening" and "way closing," and what they meant was that sometimes God opens doors or leads us by giving us a green light. And sometimes God works in our lives by closing doors or giving us a red light.

When my friends started making fun of me and quit being my friends, that was a "way closing." I think I like "way openings" better, but you can hardly miss those way closings. They're like bumping into a closed door in the middle of the night. A pretty big, can't-miss kind of "ooops." And God definitely got my attention.

I know now I want to be a forever kind of friend. A covenant friend, like Ruth was to Naomi. And I'm not mad at those girls anymore. In fact, I think I understand now. I think it was all a God thing. If they hadn't ditched me, we'd still be friends and I wouldn't have ever even *seen* the kids I've become friends with since then. I guess it feels like all the friendship spaces in my heart were filled, like when all the real estate spaces on a Monopoly board are taken, and I would have just skipped over getting to know the friends I have now. I would have missed out on *real* forever friends.

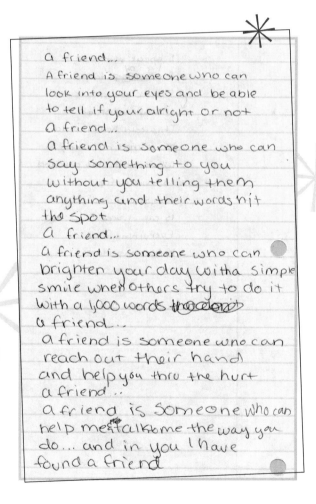

a friend...
A friend is someone who can
look into your eyes and be able
to tell if your alright or not
a friend...
a friend is someone who can
say something to you
without you telling them
anything and their words hit
the spot
a friend...
a friend is someone who can
brighten your day with a simple
smile when others try to do it
with a 1,000 words ~~thradont~~
a friend...
a friend is someone who can
reach out their hand
and help you thru the hurt
a friend...
a friend is someone who can
help me talk to me the way you
do... and in you I have
found a friend

just between god and me

To use the Quaker saying, have you had any "way openings" or "way closings"? Times when you felt a door slam in your face or an unexpected window open? What happened?

. . . .

. . . .

. . . .

. . . .

. . . .

. . . .

. . . .

. . . .

. . . .

When have you been ditched by friends, been hurt, or felt betrayed?

. . . .

. . . .

. . . .

. . . .

. . . .

. . . .

. . . .

. . . .

Now, flip it around. When have you done something just like that? Take a look at Matthew 7:1–3. Does it feel funny to think about how easy it is to justify those actions when you're not the one being hurt?

So . . . what's it going to be? How would you describe a "forever friend"? What kind of friend do you want to be?

I AM NOT A BEER CHUGGIN, POT TRIPPIN, CIGAR PUFFIN, DRUG DEALIN CHRISTIAN.

I AM A GOD LOVIN, SATAN SLAMIN, JESUS FREAKIN, WORLD CHANGIN CHRISTIAN

I AM A WARRIOR FOR CHRIST

because i love you,
i obey you,
and i will follow you . . .

i will follow you

I know that I will **always** be faced with **temptation,** but because I **love** you, I **obey** you, and I will **follow** you. . . .

—Rachel Joy Scott

From her journals, April 15, 1998

I used to think if someone was a Christian that person would automatically do things like pray and read the Bible and would automatically *not* do things like fool around and lie and cheat. But I was so wrong.

Because I became a Christian when I was really young, I wasn't old enough to have gotten into too much trouble. I hadn't had much time to "see the world" as they say. You know, get into trouble by partying, drinking, smoking—all that stuff grownups say we're not supposed to do but s-o-o-o-o-o many grownups do anyway. Well, I guess I thought when I went down the aisle at that church in Louisiana, that was that. None of that stuff would be a problem for me.

Well, again, I was so-o-o-o wrong. Like totally wrong.

Just because someone believes in Jesus doesn't make wanting wrong things go away. If anything, it just means we *know* they're wrong.

So. Gotta make a little confession. Okay. A big confession. Ready? Here goes: I started smoking.

Yeah, that's right. Me. Rachel Joy Scott. Little Miss Bible-toting, churchgoing, scripture-spouting Christian. And here's the worst part. I didn't just *try* smoking—like experimenting once or twice—I really got into it. And since you know I became a Christian when I was twelve, I can't exactly say I started smoking *before* I became a Christian. Nope, I did it with my eyes wide open, knowing full well it was against the law in Colorado and that it probably wasn't anything Jesus would go for if he were riding along beside me in my car. So now that I've probably blown your socks off, want to know the story?

I wanted to be on the edge. I didn't want to be one of those wimpy Christians who play it safe and only hang out with other Christians or "good" kids, kids who come from "good" homes, make "good" grades and never get into trouble with teachers or get detention. I *wanted* to go to parties where kids were doing stuff that would make my parents go ballistic. I *wanted* to be like Jesus when he was hanging out with those "questionable" characters that threw the religious leaders into gossip overdrive.

In fact, that was about the only thing my mom and I ever really argued about—those kinds of parties and places that she calls "worldly." (Her other favorite "mom" phrase is "high-risk factors.") She got really warped out about some of the parties I wanted to go to. But I can be pretty stubborn and persistent, and I *wanted* to be on the front lines for Jesus. But even commando teams going into combat can lose their bearings and become disoriented or lose radio communication with other members of their team. And I guess somewhere along the way I fell into the trenches. Somewhere along the way I lost radio communication.

What I mean is I was out there, on the edge, and most of my really committed Christian buddies (my Breakthrough friends) went to different schools—and my faith began to feel like a separate part of me. Walking in the hall between classes, working at Subway, staying late after school for play practice—all began to feel as far away from godly as New York is from Colorado. A big huge gap. A big black hole I'd fall into every day somewhere between the safe havens of home and church. And the raunchy, edgy, "worldly" stuff my mom would rag on me about started looking pretty good. I know it was dumb. I know it was stupid. But if humans didn't do dumb, stupid stuff on a fairly regular basis, almost nobody would ever get into trouble!

Well, anyway, I wanted to be on the front lines, I wanted to *be there,* right in the middle of everything. You know, I'm the girl who loves to make grand entrances. I'll always choose vibrant, bold colors over boring pastels, and given a choice, I'd rather go somewhere than stay home. Rather write a play than bake cookies. Rather laugh than cry.

I'm the girl who *knows* when I grow up I'm *going* places. Take planes as often as I can. Learn to drink espresso. Speak Italian. Be the first woman president of the United States . . . well . . . except for all that political stuff that goes along with it . . . .okay, forget being the first woman prez.

So, I *finally* had my driver's license, *finally* had my own car, *finally* had the chance to go and do and be with almost anyone I wanted to go and do and be with. . . . And I've thought a lot about all that and here's what I think. I think temptation isn't temptation if it's not something you really want. Like *think* about it. If you're on a diet and you don't like chocolate, then how tempting is a big piece of chocolate cake or a hot fudge sundae? If you don't like chocolate, then that stuff isn't a temptation. It's only a temptation if you *really* want it.

Other kids I know experiment with doing drugs or having sex or drinking, and all of that can have much more serious consequences, but smoking was a big deal for me—because I knew my parents would be disappointed in me. I knew it was against the law. I knew the behavior that went along with smoking wouldn't exactly be "pleasing" to God. I just flat knew it wasn't right.

But it seemed like all my drama friends smoked. I've got one friend who's got more tattoos than a redhead's got freckles—and he makes me laugh because he can be so goofy. Got another friend who says "cool, dude!" more times in one conversation than pro football players say "ya know?" in postgame interviews. Got another friend who's wacky enough to understand why I love writing poems. I know all that stuff we hear about peer pressure and "just say no" and how hard it is to stop once you start. But maybe I just got tired of always being out of it.

But what started off giving me a buzz began to really bring me down. I think there are some things that might be harder to pull out of once you get into them—like doing drugs or drinking or having sex. Once you go there, it's hard to back off, like being pulled under big waves by a powerful undertow. But I've got to tell you, backing off from smoking was hard enough, even though it started off fun and daring and kind of exciting. When it comes to smoking, what started off good ended up going bad.

The traces of smoke
the cigarette leaves,
Is a soft string of silk.
It floats thru the air thin
Creating its unpredictable path.
It seems to be pleasant to the touch
—But it is only an illusion:

Your hands and thoughts
Will never grasp its form.
The cloud of smoke
You exhale from your body
Has a solid tone of harp.
It has no appealing form
It creates no beautiful path.
It is released from your lungs
and with no lacking,
It leaves your presence.

The cigarette has deceived you
You created this beautiful image
in your mind
of the smoke that would
dance off your lips.
—But you are wrong
And like the smoke
I will leave you
Staining your
body
with
blackness
and
tar...

I think when grownups tell kids not to do things like drugs and alcohol and sex, what they *don't* tell us is that all that stuff feels good *at first* or people wouldn't keep *doing it*—at least that's what I think. I think grownups would have a lot more credibility if they owned up to that and just said, "Yeah, all that stuff can give you a good ride *at first,* but the ride can get out of control real fast and then can go real bad—worse than you can ever imagine."

Well, anyway, I started smoking and went to some parties my parents would *definitely* not have approved of and before I knew it, I was back to that feeling of two different "me's" inside. The one I *wanted* to be and the one I felt like I really was—and the two "me's" were having a major tug-of-war in the battleground of my emotions. The cigarettes, the sneaking around, the lying to my sister, the trying to be two people at once—it all started feeling ugly and yucky—and I was all torn up inside.

When people in movies play characters who are mentally ill and they say they hear voices, I think I can imagine how awful that must feel. 'Cause when I was smoking and my parents didn't know, I felt like I had an evil twin who all of a sudden would take over and I wasn't *me* anymore.

> Dear God,
>
> Haven't talked to you in awhile. I guess I've just given up. I don't know why, but it's getting to be too hard. Each day, I play the question, "Do you exist," over and over in my mind. I know you do... but even with the fact of your being, I have a hard time believing. I'm so confused... I don't know what to do. Where do you want me? What do you want? I want to be used in great ways... but I haven't the courage nor the strength. Help me through this stage of pain, through the hurt and thru the rain

And that whole thing about nicotine being addictive? Well, let me tell you, if the definition of addiction is what my teen study Bible says, "something that's not good for you at all, but that you keep needing and wanting anyway," then they're right. Because once I started smoking, I thought about it sitting in class. I thought about cigarettes when I woke up. I thought about wanting a smoke before I went to bed. I wish I could just say, "Don't go there," and you wouldn't, but I know I can't, because even if I did, you still might. Just like I did.

But you know what? God is stronger than smokes or dope or beer or anything else we can get into. I don't think God wastes anything—not our good choices and not our bad ones. I don't think any sin or dumb choice or mess-up or *anything* is bigger than God's love and forgiveness. I think Jesus was right there with me when I'd go out in the parking lot behind the Subway where I worked. Jesus was right there with me when I stood by my car in the *freezing* cold, shivering, my hands so cold I could hardly feel the cigarette in my fingers, stomping my feet to try to stay warm—just for a smoke! I think God would watch me, sigh, and say *out loud* to the angels, *"Rachel Joy Scott, don't you know I've got something better for you than this?!?"*

But when I was tired of the internal tug-of-war and all the yucky feelings, and I wanted to be *me* again, God was right there, ready and waiting to walk me through what it took to stop smoking. Ready to give me strength I didn't know I had to do the right thing—like telling my parents what I'd been doing, like asking God and my parents for forgiveness.

Okay. Picture this. If you

October 15, 98

Jesus, break these strongholds
Tear down the strings of sin
Release me from my pride
Rescue me from these games
Restore me from the hurt
Renew my heart again
Tear down this bondage
Destroy this burden
Give me love, Give me peace.
My life, my love, my wants
my needs, my passion,
My strength, my faults,
my sin, my friends,
my foes, my family,
my all... is now Yours.

had to choose between having eight teeth pulled at a dentist's office or telling a teacher you cheated on a test or having to tell your parents you'd been smoking, sneaking out, and lying about it—which one do *you* think would qualify for a Chinese torture chamber? Yeah. Try the last one. Telling my parents was no picnic. But I did it. I came clean. I asked God for the courage and the strength. And you know what? My parents were way cool. They didn't yell at me. They didn't tell me all the stuff I already knew. They didn't make me feel stupid. They just listened and hugged me. They were just *there* for me. I don't think they were really too surprised; it almost felt like they already knew somehow.

But, anyway, bottom line? It wasn't worth it. If I had it to do all over again, maybe I'd do the same thing, but I hope I wouldn't. I did learn a lot—not only about myself, but also about God and my parents. But it wasn't fun. It definitely wasn't cool. And I wouldn't recommend it.

And that friend of mine? The one who's so wise (the older one) said to me later when I told her about it, "You know, Rachel, you may have learned a lot, but you didn't learn anything that God couldn't have taught you another way." And I think she's right. Because, as I see it, if we're not supposed to sin, but we *have* to sin for God to teach us what we need to learn, then what kind of God is that? The God of double-binds? I don't think so. I don't think God would set things up that way. I think forgiveness is about making things right, not about some cosmic learning laboratory where we have to screw up to grow up.

Dec 14, 96

You said "that's bad"
I said "so what"
You said "He lies"
I said "He's fun"
You said "Please stop"
I said "Shut up"
You said "I love you"
I said "Not now"
But then the matches
Burned my hands,
And he was not there,
To care for me,
He left me,
In the dark alone,
But I was not alone,
You said, "I love you,"
I said, "Why"
You said, "Because I made you"

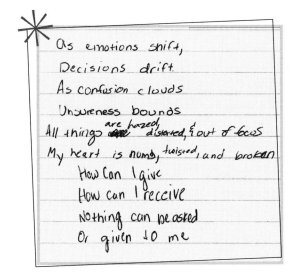

As emotions shift,
Decisions drift.
As confusion clouds
Unsureness bounds
All things are hazed, distorted, & out of focus
My heart is numb, twisted, and broken
How Can I give
How can I receive
Nothing can be asked
Or given to me

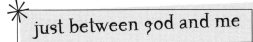

just between god and me

It happens to everybody. No matter how committed to Christ. No matter how good our intentions. No matter how hard we try. At some point, we fail God. We fail ourselves. We disappoint those we love. We make bad choices. We feel ugly and yucky inside. Confessing of our wrongdoing and having a heart willing to change are the way back from those ugly, yucky feelings.

"Grace strikes us when we are in great pain and restlessness. It strikes us when we walk through the dark valley. . . . It strikes us when we feel that our separation is deeper than usual," writes theologian Paul Tillich. Rachel knew the transforming power of God's grace because she had the courage to be honest with herself, and that honesty with herself gave her the courage to be honest with those who loved her—her parents, her friends, her youth group.

Can you let Rachel's courage give *you* courage? Courage to be honest with God and yourself? Have you ever felt separated from God? Have you ever felt that you disappointed God? Have you ever made a decision you knew was wrong but went ahead and did it anyway?

Take a moment. Let the safety and privacy of these pages be a place to come before God with honesty. Use the space that follows this prayer to write whatever comes to mind as you sit quietly.

Dear God, I'm here. It's hard to put words to what feels ugly and yucky inside. Hard to be honest about things I'd rather not think about. But I want to be honest with myself. I want to be honest with you. Jesus said, "The truth will set you free," so here's the truth, God.

April 15,98

Dear God,
I promise that I will not drink this Friday when I go out with   This is so tempting. I want to go so bad. Well, I thought about it (as you know) and I thought that since you would forgive me anyways I may as well do it. Then I realized that you will always, always forgive, but you may not let it go unpunished. Then I decided not to do it strictly out of fear. Then I thought about it more, and thought that if I did it out of fear it would not be done because I loved you, I obeyed you, and I followed you. That is my reason for not going now. I know that I will always be faced with temptation, but because I love you, I obey you, and I follow you, I will not fall into the core of it. Thank you, Father
always
Your child,
Rachel Joy

· ·

· ·

· ·

· ·

· ·

· ·

· ·

· ·

· ·

· ·

· ·

Now, is there something tempting you? Something you want to write your own "promise letter" to God about? Just remember, we are not responsible for our own transformation—that's up to God. But we allow God's transforming grace to enter our hearts by being open, willing, and honest. Tell God whatever is troubling, whatever is tempting, whatever is painful or disappointing—and then leave it in God's care. The risen Christ goes with you.

Dear God, I promise that

· ·

· ·

· ·

· ·

· ·

· ·

look hard enough
and you will always
find a light...

moments of doubt

> Look hard enough and you will always find a light...
>
> —Rachel Joy Scott
>
> From an undated journal entry

I've got a great car. A family who loves me. (Probably the order of those two ought to be reversed, but, oh well.) Friends who really care. Even though I was ditched by some friends, and that really hurt, it opened my eyes for real friends to shine through.

I've gone to most of my school dances—not with "boyfriends," but with friends who happen to be boys—so the dances aren't clammy-hands, tongue-tied, think-I'm-gonna-die kind of stressful deals. I've gone and I've had fun.

I get good grades (most of the time). People tell me I'm fun to be with, that I'm a good friend, and that I'm pretty (although I have a harder time believing that one).

So what's not to like about my life, right?

Good question. I ask myself the same thing. But sometimes—even with all that being true—I hate being me. Hate living inside my own skin. Sometimes I just hate my life.

Ever feel that way? That no matter what you do it's not good enough? That no matter how hard you try, you could have tried harder?

I know that God loves me. I know I'm forgiven. But sometimes it doesn't feel that way and sometimes, it's just not enough. And no matter how much I believe, God can feel so far away.

When I've got it so good, how can I feel so bad? Why do I feel like there's something totally wrong with me?

Some days I want to be a playwright.

Some days I *know* I'm going to be an actress.

But some days I just want to stay in bed. (My mom doesn't usually go for that, though.)

Some days I feel like I can take on the world.

Other days I don't even want to take off my covers.

Some days I feel fat and ugly, no matter what *anybody* says.

But some days I feel so alive that I can almost *taste* how good life is.

And then again, some days I just want to die.

Some days I *know* I'm going to be famous.

Other days I'm convinced I'm a certifiable loser.

So which one is the real me?

The one who's going to be famous one day or the one who feels so completely, totally weird? I flip back and forth in the way I feel about me—and you know what? I do the same thing with God. Resolute one day, doubting the next. Back and forth.

Okay, it's no surprise that I've absolutely committed my life to Christ, right? No doubt about it. Nobody has to tell me that God is God. I *know* that. I want to make a difference for God. Want to be on the front lines for God. I want my life to *matter.* But even though I *know* in my

> I've always prayed. I haven't had the best life, and I've always prayed to God that he would send me somebody who would care about me. And I just praise God for sending me an angel. In the short time that we had our friendship, Rachel made me feel like the most important person in this world. She called me her "bigger" brother.
>
> —Mark Bodiford,
> Rachel's friend

head what I believe and I *know* that God is who he says he is, even *knowing* all that, some days I don't *feel* it. I feel like God is so far away, and I wonder what's wrong with me. Some days I just want to cry, and some days praying just feels like an exercise in nothingness.

I guess I feel like my heart conspires against me—like thoughts, feelings, and doubts that aren't *really* what I think or believe take over inside. And because I've been a Christian so long, I feel even worse because I feel like I *shouldn't* feel this way, and then it just feels like I'm in a downward spiral, going down, down, and farther down.

Okay. So am I totally weird or do you feel that way, too? Do you have days when you just want to cry? Days when you're convinced you are the *ultimate* loser? Days when no matter how much you believe in God, doubts creep in around the edges? Or you get really mad at a friend for a pretty lame reason? Or you say something mean, even when you don't really mean it?

Do you ever have times when you just want to yell, *What is with me, God?* Or maybe instead of yelling at the sky, you want to whisper softly to the night, *Are you really there, God? Do you really care?*

Some days I just wonder how God can love me when I can be so on-again-off-again, so up and down. But then I remember, God's love isn't based on what *I* do. God's love is based on what *Jesus* did, but I still end up feeling like I fell into a black hole of no return.

Those feelings don't *always* collide on the same day, but on days when everything goes wrong, it's so easy to question God, too. Bad hair day. Terrible, lousy, no-good, awful, very bad days. You know, the "I hate my life" kind of days.

Well, let me tell you about one of my "I hate my life" days.

All my favorite clothes were dirty, so I had to wear a shirt and jeans I didn't like. My hair had taken on a life of its own, and I *swear* it wasn't the same hair I had the day before. My jeans felt too tight. I left my history book at home and remembered *after* I got to school that we were having an open-book quiz. *Make it through the day. That's all I have to do, just make it through the day.* But then came algebra, and of course, *that* was the day I forgot to turn my assignment sheet over, so I didn't do any of the problems on the back of the page—lost twenty-five points automatically. Too many students were using the "I forgot" excuse, so my teacher made it an auto-matic deduction of twenty-five points off the quarter grade for any "I for-got" assignments. To top it all off, I bombed on my speech in language arts—just felt like I did a really lousy job.

Can you believe it?!? I was so bummed!

My mom picked me up after school to go to the dentist. I started to tell her what a lousy day I'd had—but before I got very far, she started riding my case about how busy I've been, how I'm never home, how she's not at all surprised I forgot an assignment. As I slid down in the car seat, wishing I could just disappear, my mom said, "Rachel, you've got to take some time to catch up at home. You've got to get your room back under control. I don't know how you stand living in that mess." Yeah, right, like cleaning up my room was at the top of my list? I just wanted to go home and climb under my covers and maybe come out in about a year.

Well, anyway, bad days are just that—bad days. Even in the middle of emotional black holes like that, I know it'll get better. But doubts? Doubts about God and doubts about myself are different. Doubts aren't the kind of thing that you sleep on to make them go away. They don't go away. Doubts are persistent, nagging, niggling little intrusions into my heart and soul, like weeds taking over a garden. Left untended they just get bigger and bigger.

My mom doesn't have those kinds of days—at least she doesn't seem to 'cause she never talks about them. She's always so rock solid. My dad is like "Mr. Believer," and I can't imagine talking to him about bad days and doubts, probably because (1) he's not a girl—obviously—and I don't think guys have "fat attack" days. And (2) when I'm feeling like that, the *last* thing I want to do is have a "father/daughter" Bible study or something—and I guess that's what I think my dad would do if I ever told him how dark my feelings can be or how big my doubts can feel. I can just hear him say-ing, *Well, Rachel, I understand how you feel . . . ,* and then he'll tell me some story. Most of the time they're good stories—and I really like hearing them, because my dad's a great storyteller. But some days, I just don't want to hear it. Know what I mean?

I wish doubts about God or faith or myself were like headaches or the flu, something that you could just sleep off. But you know, I've been thinking about all this a lot lately, because I've been having some really bad days. My mom says I'm restless, edgy. I know I've had a lot going on. And I know I'm seriously in love with a guy who's one of my best friends—and he's in love with someone else—who's also one of my best friends—and I know that sounds like a soap opera, but it's true.

But anyway, after thinking about this a lot, you want to know what I think? I think doubt and faith are two sides of the same coin. I think they go together like orange juice and breakfast, friendships and fights, teenagers and music. Okay, if you think I've gone totally loony tunes, stay with me. Hear me out.

I think the deeper your commitment to God, the bigger your questions get. Maybe because the more time you spend getting to know God, the bigger the questions God figures you can handle. Or maybe . . . maybe you realize that God is not always black and white, or doesn't come with neat and tidy little answers. Maybe not everything has only one way of working out.

Like there's a story in the Gospels about this dad who has a sick daughter and she's dying. The dad runs up to Jesus to ask him to come see his daughter, because the dad knows Jesus could heal her. So Jesus basically tells the dad, "Go home. Your faith has made her well." But the dad freaks out, thinking that if Jesus doesn't actually come to his house, his daughter will die. This dad just can't quite buy the possibility of a "remote" healing option. So he *believes* Jesus can heal her, but he *doubts* the way Jesus is going to do it. There it is—faith and doubt. Right there together. Almost in the same breath.

So I figure, when I'm filled with doubt and confusion or I'm feeling lonely and sad, but I'm praying and telling God about it, I'm still *believing* 'cause I'm talking to God, right? I mean, if you're talking to God, even if you're asking God if he really exists, some part of you believes he does—or you wouldn't be asking, right?

So anyway, this dad says, "Lord, I believe. Help my unbelief!" There it is again! Belief and unbelief. That dad believed—and didn't believe. Go figure!

Well, even though sometimes I don't want my dad to tell me what the Bible says, here's a cool thing he told me about the Bible. He says there's this thing called "oral tradition" that is partly how the Bible was written. What he says is that a long time ago, not many people knew how to read or write. So most ordinary people couldn't read—in fact, there weren't even any books or Bibles. The only way people knew the teachings of God was by hearing the same stories over and over again, kind of like when we play the same songs over and over until we learn all the words. So I figure when someone realized all these stories about Jesus *needed* to be written down, that if a story was told over and over enough times for it to be one of the ones that got written down, then it must be pretty important. So, "Lord, I believe. Help my unbelief," must be a way of saying belief and unbelief go together.

I think my most common "unbeliefs" are—

* That I'm unlovable.
* That I'm not good enough.
* That no one will ever love me—not like a friend—but really love me.
* That something's wrong with me when God feels far away.

Dear God,
why do I feel dry in your Spirit? why do I feel that the fire has died within me, yet so many claim they see the light of you, oh God, burning brightly? why do I have to feel moments of doubt, distrust, disbelief, stages of anger, & stages of loneliness when it comes to you, Father? why do I lose focus of you during praise & worship as well as prayer? Why can't I completely be consumed by you? Why can't I be used by you? Why do I feel self-righteous at times? Why do I feel afraid?

Father,
    I'm sorry. I'm sorry I ever doubted you. I'm sorry I didn't trust you. You know what your doing and you know what's best for me. For now on, I put all faith and trust in you
            In Jesus Name;
                Amen
    Rachel Joy

You know, I even wrote a song, only to realize *after* writing the song that it says what I *don't* believe! Between the two, given a choice, I like belief much better than unbelief, whether it's unbelief about God or me. But the way I see it, God must be bigger than any doubt, any despair, any dark feelings I can have—because if God isn't bigger than my feelings, then how can God be God?

Satan's Lie has now become the song of the world

I'm slowly dying
I'm fading away
I'm losing control
I'm slowly dying
There is nothing left to say
There is nothing left to hold

I'm slowly dying
Just a memory
I'm slowly dying
Nothing left of me

Oh when I look into your eyes
and you look back at me
You see nothing beautiful
There is nothing good about me

I'm slowly dying
I'm losing the faith
That I had as a child
I can't find my way
Can't seem to find it

On my soul is being ripped apart
and no one seems to care
About this achy feeling in my heart
And mind is about to tear

I'm slowly dying
Can some one save me?
Can some one help now?
I'm slowly dying
It's such a tragedy,
Can't it all stop now?

I'm slowly dying
Just a memory
I'm slowly dying
Nothing left of me.

~ I wrote this today and realized that
this is the way the world feels... don't
ever sing this song... it is Satan's lie.

Oalways... your little sis,

Rachel Joy

just between god and me

How about it? What are your most common "unbeliefs"? Those yucky
things you think and feel when you're having one of those "I-hate-my-life"
terrible, awful, lousy, no-good, very bad days?

Read Romans 8:38. What do you think God would say about your unbeliefs? How would God "rewrite" those unbeliefs?

Things untold
Things unseen
One day all these things
Will come to me.

Life of meaning
Life of hope
Life of significance
Is mine to cope.

I have a purpose
I have a dream
I have a future
So it seems

desire is
not selfish . . .
desire is part of
dreaming

all i want in life

> All I want in life is a camera with endless black and white film, a paint set with hundreds of blank canvasses, a piano to write my own music, and a plane ticket. It sounds like a lot, but how much is it compared to everything most people have. I was never a princess. Growing up, I wanted many things but never received them. Desire is not selfish. I desire many things, but I don't get them. Desiring is part of dreaming.
>
> —Rachel Joy Scott
>
> From an undated journal entry

I like vintage clothes and vanilla candles, cool night air, and my dog's snowy white fur. My room stays messy despite my best efforts to keep it clean. And no matter how hard I try to keep things picked up, clothes literally disappear into the black hole under my bed.

I like my brothers' quirks, Craig's "to do" lists, and my sister's sense of humor. I like hanging out with my friends and making funny faces. I like driving anywhere, getting a new CD, making my mom laugh, and realizing the first line of a poem is running through my mind.

I *don't* like designer clothes, cooked carrots, headaches, itty-bitty type in textbook footnotes, burnt marshmallows, and the "pretty but dumb" stigma for women. I can't stand being late, music playing in doctors' offices, or feeling behind in homework.

And I know exactly what I want to be when I grow up—most days anyway. I want to be famous. I want people all over the world to know me. The only question is *how* I'm going to be famous.

Sometimes I wish I could live five different lives. In the first life I'd be an actress. Second, I'd be an incredibly talented writer. Third, I'd go for being a great American playwright. Fourth, I'd want to be the successor to Amy Grant, a Christian pop star—diva and songwriter all in one. But somewhere in there I also want to be an American missionary, living someplace exotic like Albert Schweitzer did.

I can't see myself getting married. Can't see myself *ever* "settling down." Can't see myself ever being *pregnant* and having babies.

One November, my family went to Indiana to spend Thanksgiving with our family back there. All my cousins, aunts, uncles—everyone—decided to go shopping. But we didn't head for the mall. We headed for our favorite kinds of places—the secondhand stores. Goodwill. Salvation Army. Thrift shops. It was so cool.

At Goodwill, I found the coolest old wedding dress, and I really wanted to try it on. My mom said I could, but with only two dressing rooms and a huge Goodwill store, I had to wait a long time for my turn. But once I got my shot at the dressing room, I did the whole deal—veil, dress, everything. It was so cool! I came out of the dressing room—instant Goodwill bride—and modeled for everyone. Not only did my family think it was great (they took about a zillion pictures!), people came from all over the store to see the "show"! It was the best. Way better than I'd bargained for. Everyone clapped. Everyone was smiling, laughing, having a great time that day in a musty, filled-with-stuff-somebody-wanted-to-get-rid-of Goodwill store. I felt like I was a star. I think that's as close as I'll ever get to being a bride, because, you know, somehow that moment just seemed complete.

My mother has always told me I'm unique. She says I'm different from

> Rachel was so excited and insistent that we wait for her to try this dress on. It took her a few minutes, and when she stepped out from the curtain, I remember thinking how beautiful Rachel made that old, dingy wedding dress look. I took a picture of her with flowers and all. She took some bows and proudly went back in the dressing room to change.
>
> —Beth Nimmo, Rachel's mom

the rest of my family. Special. She says that before I was even born, when she was pregnant with me, a minister prayed over her and told her, "There will be something different, something special about this child."

My dad says he always thought that meant he'd finally get a boy. But nope, I turned out very much a girl. My mom called me and my sisters Chuck, George, and Henry . . . and I was Henry. That way Dad got to have his "boys."

But sometimes I do feel different from others. Sometimes I feel like my life is going to be anything but ordinary—even though most days my life's v-e-r-y ordinary.

But still, growing up I had baby dolls and Barbie dolls and played what other girls played. But it was more because I just wanted to be a part of what everyone else was doing. I didn't want to be left out. What I really loved doing were things like charades or Pictionary or card games, the kind of stuff where you had to use strategy to outwit other players. I think I'd be really good at playing chess, but I've never learned. But maybe, someday, I'll get someone to teach me.

Anyway, give me a chance to outwit or out-think or out-strategize someone else, and I'm jazzed. Once I start playing Charades, I honestly think I can outlast any player, anytime, anywhere.

But it's not just that I liked playing mind games when other girls liked playing dolls that makes me think I'm different somehow. It's just that sometimes I *feel* different. I don't know. It's just a feeling I have, deep down inside me. I have a funny feeling (not funny like "ha ha," but funny like weird), a kind of inner sense that my life is going to be different, unusual, or that I'm going to do something important. Sometimes I feel like that funny feeling comes from God. Other times, I don't know. I just think I'm strange. But who knows? I guess the answer to that is—only God.

But back to wanting to be an actress, a writer, a songwriter, a mission-ary, and all the other stuff I daydream about . . . I guess if I want to do *all* of those things, that means I don't really know *what* I want to do. But I know I want to live big. I want to laugh big. I want to love big. I want life to know I was here. Leave my mark. And somehow make a difference in the process.

I think about the future a lot. Daydream. Imagine. Hope. Wishful thinking. I think those are all different kinds of prayer, at least for me. Writing to God in my journal is praying. And when I'm daydreaming, writing poems, journaling, or just imagining what might be, I don't think small, I don't wish small, I don't think "ordinary." I like to think big, dream big, live big.

Now that I think about it, I don't know exactly what I want to *do* when I grow up, but I know what I want to *be*.

Days of routine are killing me
I'm in a censored box of reality
When can I unlock the door and see
The path that leads to my destiny

Don't put limits on what I can do
I have faith, why can't you
I wanna show the world what I have
I won't be labled as average

Don't keep me from my dreams
I can reach them if I believe
One day the world will see
What I know burns inside of me

I have the strength, I have the faith
I have the talent, I will concentrate
I will go beyond your expectations
Past all bounds and limitations

I want to be one who speaks truthfully, no matter what the cost.

I want to be one who acts with tolerance, compassion, and love as my top three guides for any decision I make.

I want to be one who follows my heart and listens for God in the smallest of moments and biggest of choices.

I want to be one who is grace-full and gratitude-filled.

I want to be one who sees in every day what I have and all I've been given rather than be blinded by what I don't have.

Standing at a crossroad,
Two paths to take,
Expected to choose
The path to my fate.

If it's all the same
to you, world...
Neither is my choice.
It's always one right
after another,
And choosing is annoyance.

Why not stand here
at the fork in the road,
And let my mind
Create the stories unfold.

I want to be one who trusts that God is enough—and God has made me enough. Good enough, smart enough, strong enough for whatever God calls me to be.

I want to open my arms wide and embrace life in all of its goodness and all of its badness because I believe the good outweighs the bad—for always and ever.

I want to remember to breathe deeply and sing loudly and love passionately and believe absolutely and see fully what's really important.

And I think I'll leave the particulars of how and when and where I'm going to be and do all of that to God—I think God is big enough to handle it all.

just between god and me

What are your dreams? If you could live five lives, what would they be and why?

. . . .

. . . .

. . . .

. . . .

. . . .

. . . .

. . . .

. . . .

. . . .

. . . .

. . . .

. . . .

. . . .

Spend a few minutes reading this verse from Deuteronomy. Read the words slowly. Read it more than once. Read it softly, but out loud, like a quiet prayer. Then spend a few minutes reflecting on what these words say to you.

I HAVE SET BEFORE YOU LIFE AND DEATH, BLESSINGS AND CURSES. CHOOSE LIFE . . . LOVING THE LORD YOUR GOD, OBEYING HIM, AND HOLDING FAST TO HIM; FOR THAT MEANS LIFE TO YOU . . .
—DEUTERONOMY 30:19–20

When you're faced with decisions about your future, when you think about your hopes and dreams, what does the phrase "choose life" mean to you? In what ways can you "choose life" in your life right now? What is "life giving" to you and what is "life taking"? What choices make you feel good about being you? What choices make you feel bad?

Proverbs 1

What I'm Learning:

1. to attain & acquire a life of wisdom & discipline
2. to understand & apply words of insight
3. to do what is right, just, & fair
4. to give wisdom to the simple _one who moral direction and inclined to evil_
5. to give knowledge & guidence to the young
6. to let the wise listen & add to their learning
7. to let the discerning get guidence
8. to understand proverbs & parables
9. to understand sayings & riddles of the wise
10. to become a better intellect of the Word

✳Proverbs 1:7 "The fear of the Lord is the
　　　　　　beginning of knowledge,
　　　　　　but fools despise wisdom
　　　　　　& discipline."

fear: to respect highly

What I am learning?

. . . .

. . . .

. . . .

. . . .

. . . .

. . . .

. . . .

. . . .

Up this lonely, dusty road,
I will find You.
Past the shallow and the cold,
I will find You.
Through this city's horrid fears,
Beyond the stream of fallen tears,
Over the mountain of endless hate,
Past this hell's dark, heavy gate,
I will find You,
I will find You,
I will find You and Your love.

you have to make
room for him.
a lot of room.

whatever it takes

> God can't do anything in your life unless you meet him halfway. You have to make room for him. A lot of room.
>
> —Rachel Joy Scott
>
> From a chapter titled "What do I do about God?"
> from a book Rachel was in the process of writing

something you need to know about this chapter—

Rachel had completed two chapters for a book she was writing. She titled the chapters, "What do I do about God?" and "What do I do about my family?" Once she began spring play rehearsals, she struggled with time limitations and fatigue and made no progress on the manuscript beyond the initial two chapters. However, those two chapters, in addition to the numerous poems, song lyrics, essays, and short stories found scattered throughout her room and tucked into random notebooks, form the basis from which much of the narrative in this book is adapted.

What follows in the first half of this chapter is a short story Rachel wrote and titled "Gloves of Conviction." Rachel typed this short story rather than writing it in longhand but not, apparently, for a school project or any required assignment. She wrote "Gloves of Conviction" simply because she was deeply affected by a simple encounter with two strangers. The short story appears here with only minor editing.

What follows the short story is an excerpt from one of the two chapters she *wrote, and appears to be what Rachel considered most important in learning to "walk the talk." Again, she typed this work rather than writing it out longhand, and her words are published with minimal editing. Unlike the first-person narrative in the preceding chapters, a story-like narrative adapted and developed from her journals, this chapter is all Rachel. Rachel wanted to know God. She took her faith seriously. And Rachel wanted others to do the same. If some of this chapter sounds a little "preachy," well, just know it's not a grownup putting words in Rachel's mouth—these words are straight from the typed pages she left behind. From a girl that liked "vintage" clothes, these words are "vintage" Rachel: straightforward, uncompromising, direct, and to the point.*

Okay. New topic. Got to tell you about what happened one day at work.

After school and weekends I work at a Subway sandwich shop just a few blocks from my house. My friends come in a lot to see me and hang out. It's actually a pretty cool place.

So one Sunday I was opening the store, which meant I came in about 9 A.M. and had about two hours of work to do by myself. On Sundays, no other employee comes in until around 11 A.M. and usually no customers come in till about 11:30, so I always have plenty of time on my hands.

That day I couldn't believe how windy and cloudy it was. The cold of the breeze alone could give you chills. At 10 A.M. I flipped the switch for the "Open" sign and unlocked the doors. Must have been only five minutes later that I heard the doorbell ringing, telling me I had a customer. I went out front and began to put the gloves on, ready to make the first sandwich of the day. When I looked up, I saw a woman who must have been in her late forties. She was wearing several layers of clothes that were torn and dirty. Her face was dark from dirt. She was shivering and began to cough in an almost uncontrollable manner. When she stopped coughing, she looked up at me and gave me a warm smile.

"What can I do for you, ma'am?" I asked.

"Oh, I was just wondering if you happen to know what time the buses come," she said pleasantly. "I have been waiting out in the cold for the bus for two hours. You think they wouldn't be so late, especially on a Saturday."

I felt really bad for her when I told her it was actually Sunday. She looked at me with such embarrassment and shock.

"Oh no," she said, dismayed. "I need to get back downtown. I thought it was Saturday. Well, do you mind if I just sit here awhile till I figure out what to do?"

"No problem," I told her and she sat at the table in the far corner of the store. As I looked at her and thought about her situation more carefully, I realized that she must have been poor, maybe even homeless. She was dressed in the dingiest clothes that hadn't been washed in a while. She had a snug, winter hat on, three layers of baggy, flannel pants, tennis shoes that were worn through, and cheap gloves that were turned inside out with fringes coming off all sides.

I felt right then and there that I should make her a sandwich free of charge, that I should talk to her . . . tell her that whatever she did, God loved her and wanted her to trust in him. I knew where all this was coming from. I knew God was giving me these words and asking me to go talk to her. But what if . . . what if . . . the usual questions and doubts about why I shouldn't crowded in, and I didn't say any of what I was thinking, what I wanted to say.

I went back to work, trying to forget about it—trying to forget about her . . . hoping she would leave soon.

My next customer, a well-dressed woman in her early thirties, came in about an hour later. She had her hair pulled up nicely and was wearing perfume. I made her sandwiches and we were at the cash register when she asked me how long that woman had been sitting there.

"About an hour," I said.

"Did she get anything to eat?" she asked me.

"No. She was waiting for the bus, thinking today was Saturday. She came in here after a couple of hours when she got too cold to wait outside. She needs to get back downtown, but I don't think she knows what she's going to do."

The lady asked if I would mind making one more sandwich. I just looked at her and smiled. I never made a sandwich with such happiness and guilt at the same time. I told the lady no charge and handed her a bag of chips to go with it. She thanked me, walked over to the other woman, handed her the food and began to talk with her. They must have talked for two hours before I saw them leave.

As I was cleaning the tables, feeling bad for not talking to the first woman myself, I noticed she had left her gloves. I picked the gloves up, sat down, and started praying. I felt like I had passed up the chance to do something for God. But when I started praying and telling God how I felt, how sorry I was that I had ignored the opportunity to tell that woman about his love, I felt God answer me right there, sitting at a table in Subway. As I was holding the pair of gloves left behind by a woman I'll probably never see again, I felt God was telling me something that will always give me a boldness in other situations when I have the chance to speak up for God.

It's funny to try to put words to what you feel like God is telling you, because it's so *inside,* but here's what I felt God was saying to me in that moment: *You feel like she missed something because you didn't speak up, but she didn't lose anything. The other woman is sharing with the poor woman right now and she will not lose out on me. You lost. You passed up the chance to gain something. You just let a wonderful flame pass by you and into the hands of another. Know this, child of mine, when you do not follow through with the boldness and knowledge I have given you—you are affected more than the other person is.*

Well, those gloves became gloves of conviction to me. I realized I had missed an opportunity, but by the grace of God, I wasn't going to miss another one. I decided that when I had little inside nudges, I was going to pay attention. If I felt like God was telling me to write a friend a letter, I was going to write the letter—and not worry about the outcome. If I felt an inner nudge to call a friend, I was going to call a friend. I wasn't going to miss out on another chance to tell somebody about God.

If there's anything I learned that day cleaning off a dirty table at a Subway shop, I learned this: God is ever present, ever caring, ever leading me in ways to make a difference. God cares about a poor, confused old lady who needed a sandwich and a ride. God cares about me. I guess what it all comes down to is commitment. Am I going to take God seriously or not? Is God worthy of a commitment to last a lifetime? Is God worthy of my everything? I think so.

At first, after that lady left the Subway shop, I was so hard on myself for not doing what I felt God had "nudged" me to do. Then I realized God would use this in my life just like every other experience—to teach me

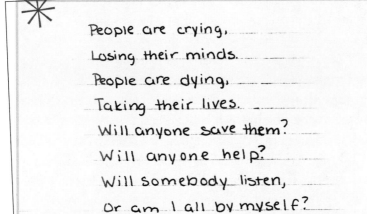

People are crying,
Losing their minds.
People are dying,
Taking their lives.
Will anyone save them?
Will anyone help?
Will somebody listen,
Or am I all by myself?
Please reach out your hand,
Grab a hold of their life.
Don't let go,
Without a good fight.
Witness to them,
Show them the way.
Give them God's love,
And give it today.

more about his heart and how to obey his voice. So I wrote down what I thought God was teaching me; I started writing some of the things I felt I was learning. And well, here goes. Some of this may sound kinda hard, but if that verse in Philippians is true, you know, the one about God beginning "a good work in you" and bringing it to "completion," then that means God is helping me learn to know him.

So, if you want to know God, there are certain things you've just gotta do. It's hard, but it's not *that* hard. Let's take it from the top:

I. **you've got to get involved in a church with a good youth group.** It has to be a place where you can really grow spiritually. Somewhere you can get to know God. Once you find a church you like, really listen to what is being taught, because in church, you learn about God. (I mean, the people up there in front have done a lot more studying the Bible and thinking about God than I have, so probably they've got some things to say that are worth hearing.)

I know sometimes it's hard to pay attention, but ask God to help you listen. Ask God to help you hear what you need to hear. In fact, sometimes I don't even sit with my friends if I think they will distract me. I know that sounds hard, but if I am distracted, how am I going to know that I'm not missing something I need to hear? I challenge you to listen and see what

Hey,

I'm probably going to write a lot since I have no more friends. I was talking to Lori about everything. She's so cool. She motivated me to start reading my Bible and so I started with John. I read a chapter a night. I have this journal where I write down verses that stand out ~~~~ in my mind or that could help me in witnessing. Then I write a brief summary of the chapter so I know that I am REALLY reading it and know what ~~~~ is going on.

Always,
Rachel Joy

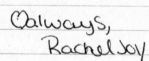

God will do. Take a risk. Chance it. Trust God. Watch to see what God is doing. God won't let you down.

2. it's good to read the bible. Don't go straight through, but start with something like the Book of John. I have a daily Bible and I love it.

I can think of a lot of reasons not to read the Bible. It uses weird words. It can be boring. It's not always easy to understand. The people in the Bible have names and live in places that would *never* make it on prime time TV.

But here's why reading the Bible (and going to church) is so important. I think reading the Bible does for me spiritually what eating does physically. Here's what I mean. Everyone tells us how important it is to read the Bible if you're a Christian, just like everyone tells us how important it is to eat right. But if you don't read the Bible, just like if you don't eat right, nothing shows up right away. Nothing seems any different. You don't look different right away. Don't act any different. Whether you do or you don't doesn't seem to make much difference in any way that's visible— at least not right away.

But when I eat, when I swallow and the food goes into my digestive system, then my stomach goes to work and does stuff with it—stuff I don't want to know. Well, that's kinda like what God does in our souls. We pick up a Bible and open it—that's like opening the fridge and deciding what looks good. Then we read the words and the words float around in our brains—that's like food getting to our stomachs. Then God does something in our souls—like our stomachs do something with food while we aren't really even paying attention or aware it's happening.

The Book of John—21 days of John
- ☑ chapter 1 - day 1   4/21
- ☑ chapter 2 - day 2   4/22
- ☑ chapter 3 - day 3   4/24 4/26
- ☑ chapter 4 - day 4   4/24 4/26
- ☑ chapter 5 - day 5   4/26
- ☑ chapter 6 day 6   4/26
- ☐ chapter 7 day 7
- ☐ chapter 8 day 8
- ☐ chapter 9 day 9
- ☐ chapter 10 day 10
- ☐ chapter 11 day 11
- ☐ chapter 12 day 12 5/2
- ☐ chapter 13 day 13
- ☐ chapter 14 day 14
- ☐ chapter 15 day 15
- ☐ chapter 16 day 16
- ☐ chapter 17 day 17
- ☐ chapter 18 day 18
- ☐ chapter 19 day 19
- ☐ chapter 20 day 20
- ☐ chapter 21 day 21

John 1

1:1 - In the begining was the word, and the word was with God, and the Word was God.

1:5 - And the light shines in the darkness, and the darkness did not Comprehend it.

1:23 I am a voice of one crying in the wilderness, 'make straight the way of the Lord.'

1:29 Behold, the Lamb of God who takes away the sin of the world!

In this Chapter, John shows his true love for God by being selfless and giving God his Glory. He then baptizes Jesus, and a dove descends from the Heavens, symbolizing the Spirit. Then Andrew and another who followed Jesus. Andrew went to his brother and told him of the messiah. Jesus then meets Simon and changes his name to Peter The next day Philip and Nathanael follow Christ. Jesus then knew that Nathaneal was going to follow him. Before Nathanael had a chance to tell him.

Breakthru - I Corinthians 3:12-21   4/22
            - Proverbs 23:7
            - Luke 2:34,35
            - Hebrews 12:12,13
            - 2 Corinthinians 10:2-5
            - Hebrew 12:1
            - James 4:7,8
            - Phillipians 4:6-9
            - 1 John 1:9
            - John 17:15

John 2
2:16 "Take these things away; stop making
    my Father's house a house of merchandise
    (~~Bazaar~~)

In this chapter, Jesus goes to a wedding
where they run out of wine. He changes
water to wine. The He goes to the temple
where people are selling things and are
making money, so he overturns their tables.
He tells them to destroy the temple, and
.hat He will raise it up in 3 days. He
was referring to his death and ressurection
But they did not know this.

4:32,34 I (Jesus) have food to eat that you do not know about. (34) My food is to do the will of Him who sent me, and to accomplish His work.

4:42 It is no longer because of what you (a believer) said that we believe, for we have heard for ourselves and know that this One is indeed the Savior of the world.

4:46-54 Jesus heals a man's son. This man was only going to truly believe that Jesus was the Son of God if he saw evidences and miracles. Jesus told him and then told him his son was healed. Jesus only had to speak the words of healing, and it was fulfilled

John 5

5:1-9 In Jerusalem there was a pool, and once a year the diseased, sick, and lame would gather by this pool. This angel would stirr the water.

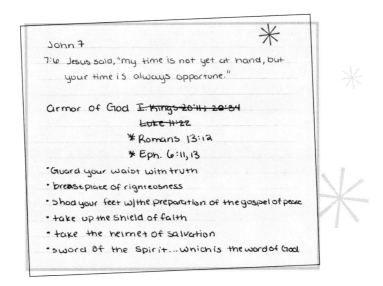

I used to always read those Christopher Pike books. You know, the horror ones. But now, I don't. My favorite book in the whole world is the Bible. I have a daily Bible and a teen Bible. I love to read it, but I didn't always. I would be on and off with reading it. Whenever I had the time or felt like it, I would pick it up and skim over a couple of verses. But then, a while back, I was encouraged to start reading the Book of John. So, I read a chapter a night. But this time, I started writing down important verses in a notebook. Then when I finished reading, I would go back and write down a few paragraphs summarizing what I just read. I think people tend to read with their eyes shut. What I mean by that is, when you read, it's important to *really* read. Don't just read through it as quickly as you can, but read to understand what it is really saying. I've learned so much by reading the Bible. I want to go out and tell people about it. I also read books about the Bible and God and that helps, too.

3. start keeping a quiet time. What is a quiet time? A quiet time is the easiest thing in the world to understand. All it is is you spending time with God. I usually have mine at night, but I think most people have their quiet times in the morning (don't ask me why I think that; I just do). But put it into your schedule; set a certain time.

I love quiet times. I usually go in my room, put on some Christian music, and talk to God. I like to read my Bible during my quiet times. Do what is comfortable for you. There are no rules. I started with ten or fifteen minutes a day, and soon I didn't even look at the clock. After you get going, time won't matter. Sometimes, I've gone up to forty-five minutes in my quiet times. But don't feel like you HAVE to do this or that—just do whatever you want, but spend time with God.

I like to take walks a lot of the time or go somewhere like my room so I won't be bothered. One time I just got up and began to dance to the music I had playing. God became so much more personal when I started doing things like this. I got to know him and let him get to know me.

Until I started doing my quiet times in ways that I actually enjoyed, I never seemed to *get* it. I would always begin like this: I'd read my Bible and try to pray and it worked for the first couple of weeks, but then I'd get lazy and make excuses why I couldn't do it that night. But when I decided to start having my quiet time by doing things I really enjoyed and decided to stick with it, it became easier. If it is part of your schedule, just like brushing your teeth and washing your hands, it's easier to keep it up.

4. prayer is so important. Prayer is your tool to answers. If you want God to put things in your life and you want answers, you have to talk to God. You have to ask. You have to make room for God. A lot of room. If you do this, things will begin to happen. God will talk to you. I mean it. He will. It was just a few weeks ago that I actually heard God. I mean heard God as if he were standing there before me.

I have never experienced anything like that. God had given me words and feelings and signs before, but he had never talked to me like that. I think I only heard God's voice because I sought God diligently, on a regular basis, whether I felt like it or not. I had my ups and downs and I fell a few times, but I did not give up.

Don't give up, because God's reward is worth it all. Whatever it takes, do it. Seek God with a whole heart. Love God with a passion. And don't give the excuse "I am just a teenager," or "I'll do that when I grow up," because it doesn't work that way. God wants to know you NOW. I could sit here and tell you what to do and what to say, but where will that get you? Go after God. Trust me . . . but better yet . . . trust God. Christianity is not a label but a lifestyle.

Once you start doing these four things, you begin to explore God and all of his possibilities. You develop a relationship with God. A person can know everything there is to know *about* God, but that doesn't mean that person *knows* God. But doing these things, you can and you will. You will take what once was a label and make it a lifestyle.

I can't emphasize how important these things are. I hear so many of my friends complain about how they don't have time. If I think I don't have time for God then I am too busy. And being too busy is the most lame excuse I've ever heard. I want to be more willing than that. God can't do anything in my life—or yours—unless we're willing to meet God halfway. After you start doing these things, everything will fall into place. You will see what God can do with a willing heart.

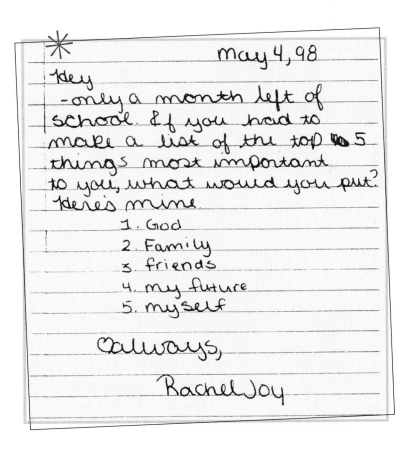

may 4, 98

Hey
-only a month left of
school. If you had to
make a list of the top 5
things most important
to you, what would you put?
Here's mine

1. God
2. Family
3. friends
4. my future
5. myself

Always,

Rachel Joy

the top 5 things most important to me

Okay, being ABSOLUTELY HONEST, my top 5 are (it's okay to list shopping, music, or boys first. . . . This is where being honest counts):

1. . . . .
2. . . . .
3. . . . .
4. . . . .
5. . . . .

But what I WISH my top 5 were:

1. . . . .
2. . . . .
3. . . . .
4. . . . .
5. . . . .

He gave His life... for me • I will... give my life to Him.
JESUS CHRIST
He's got the whole world in His Hands. He's got the whole world in His Hands. He's got the whole world in His Hands. He's got the whole wide world in His Hands.
What if you were to die today? What would happen to you? Where would you go? Tommorrow is not a promise, but a chance. It may not be there for you. After death, then what? Where will you spend your Eternity? Will you have an eternal life with our Loving Father, or will you be ripped from the arms of your Savior Jesus Christ. ETERNITY IS IN YOUR HANDS... CHANGE IT!

if being a christian
were easy,
everyone would
do it.

ten

always in christ

> If being a **Christian** were **easy,** everyone would do it. **Not** to **know God,** but to have the easy **life.**
>
> —Rachel Joy Scott
>
> From a chapter titled, "What do I do about God?"
> from a book Rachel was in the process of writing

April 20, 1999

Overslept. As usual.

Stayed up late last night working on a play I'm writing for next year. Don't know why, but my favorite time to sit at the computer and write is when everyone else has gone to bed. The house is all quiet except for clocks ticking, the refrigerator humming, and the furnace running. So I stayed up late, thinking, writing, reading, praying. Late night is my time.

My mom's really worried that I'm getting way too tired—and I did sleep all day Sunday. Literally *all* day. I really *was* tired. I read in a magazine article that if you have to use an alarm clock to wake up every morning, then you're sleep deprived. So . . . every kid I know must be sleep deprived!

We just finished with our spring play about ten days ago. With play rehearsals almost every day after school, and the long hours for the performances, well, I think I pushed the sleep deprivation for an average American teenage kid to the limit. I've been staying up even later than usual to keep up with homework (which I don't think I've done too well lately . . . I've really got to hit the books!). Well, with all that, I *have* been really tired. But by the end of the school year, I'm always tired. Anyway, even being really tired, I *still* stay up late. Drives my mom crazy. I can just hear her . . . *Rachel, if you couldn't get out of bed this morning, you've got to go to bed earlier tonight.*

But I don't, especially on Monday nights. I work at Subway after school and then go to my youth group—so I always have a late night on Mondays. Which means Tuesday mornings I'm *never* the first one out of bed. By the time I heard my mom knocking on my door the second time saying, "Rachel, come on. You've got to get up right away," I knew I had to get moving. So my feet hit the floor, I threw on a black tank top and a pair of dark running pants, grabbed a long-sleeved plaid shirt, and headed upstairs to my mom's bathroom.

My mom and I kinda have this "thing" on school mornings. I always use her makeup. I think it started because I, well, I *have* my own make-up—I just can't ever *find* my own makeup. You know, it's kind of all over the place . . . in my backpack . . . in my locker or sometimes I leave it in my car (a little red Acura), which I charmed my stepdad into getting for me, although it didn't take too much charming because he and my mom were getting pretty tired of having to drive me and my brothers all over the place! I think that's the *real* reason my mom finally let me get my driver's license! Anyway, my makeup never seems to be where I can find it first thing in the morning. (Hey! Give me a break! My first class starts at 7:15!)

So on school days I throw on my clothes, head up to my mom's room, and use *her* makeup. I think it must be a "mom thing"—moms always put stuff back where it goes. I wonder if that's related to hormonal changes that come with pregnancy or something, because it's going to take some special hormone or a miracle for *me* to ever do that!

Sometimes my mom pretends to be a little aggravated at me when I use her makeup, but I don't think she really minds (as long as I put it back where it goes!). And sometimes we play this wacky little game where we switch roles. My mom will act like the kid and I'll act like the mom. It's really pretty funny. My mom mimics me or my brothers and then we say what my mom would usually say—and then we just end up laughing. Anyway, this morning before I flew out the door of my mom's room, I said, "Mom! I just don't know what I'm going to do with you!" She just grinned at me. I glanced at the clock, realized we were cutting it close, and yelled at my brother Craig to get in gear so we wouldn't be late. So much for a typical school morning at our house!

Even though I get mad at Craig for almost *always* being late, I really do like driving to school with him. In Colorado, it's almost always cold when we leave for school. Frost or snow on the windshield. Have to start the car and let it get warm. Scrape the windshield. Drive to school on streets lined with white sidewalks, white trees, white yards covered with snow. We always park in Clement Park, next to the high school, grab our backpacks, and walk along an icy trail to the front entrance of the school. Of course, we *never* hassle with trying to remember gloves (who's awake enough at 7 A.M. to think of that?!), so our hands are freezing when we walk through the big doors of the high school. Every morning we just say "C-ya," before Craig goes one way down the hall and I head the other way. Even when I've been really mad at Craig about something (usually being late), we still say "C-ya," when we walk through those doors.

But, made it to class on time. *B-O-R-I-N-G.* Only five more weeks of school. Yeah! And then I did what I always do when I'm bored in class. Wrote in my journal (it's a great trick for when you really don't want to pay attention, because teachers always think you're taking notes and they're so impressed!), drew some doodles, and watched the clock. Endured first period. Survived second period. Third period was my favorite—forensics. But I confess, I sat at my desk drawing and doodling even in my favorite class. But I like to show my forensics teacher my poems and drawings. She thinks they're really good. Today I drew a picture of eyes and tears and a rose growing out of a columbine plant. Don't know why. Just felt tired and sad and didn't really want to concentrate on the class assignment. I think spring fever is hitting hard.

But I haven't just been bored. I've been restless, edgy. Kinda down. Don't really know what's wrong with me. I know I got really mad at one of my best friends and we had this horrible fight about writing a play for next year—a really stupid argument. But it's not just that. It's something I can't explain or put words to. I just have these weird feelings and when I write poems, even I'll admit they sound terribly sad—but I don't feel *that* sad! I'm just, I don't know. Lonely, I guess. Ready for school to be out for summer. Ready to sleep late, go to work, and hang out with friends. I think I need to give my brain and bod a rest.

For quite a while I'd been noticing a boy who was always alone. He often seemed kinda sad and bummed out. He's a special needs student—has a bunch of physical disabilities that just make life so complicated for him. Well, he always seemed to have to fend for himself. He was never surrounded by any friends. Anyway, even though I've been feeling tired and restless and weird, this guy got my attention. I guess I felt like if I had so much going for me, and every day was such a struggle for me—he must *really* feel tired and restless and weird—and lonely, too. So, that bugged me. Just because he couldn't talk like everyone else, just because he was *different,* it made me mad that other kids acted like he was invisible. So I decided that *had* to change. After I'd been noticing him for weeks, saying "hi" to him in the halls, speaking to him at lunch (just, you know, *normal* stuff), I started wondering if he'd ever been on a date. My guess was, probably not! So? I decided I was going to make it happen. Walked right up to him and just about knocked his socks off.

"Jim, have you ever had a date?" I asked him.

"No," he said, *so* embarrassed.

"Well, then I am asking you for a date. Would you have dinner and go to a movie with me?" I asked.

Wow! Did he ever shine! His whole face lit up. It was amazing. Such a simple thing, but I guess not for him. I mean, I was afraid he was going to lose his balance and fall over in the hall or something. Anyway, we didn't set the actual date; too much stuff was going on to set it up right then. But, we have a date coming up—and it felt so good to do something *so* simple for someone. All I did was ask a lonely guy if he wanted to hang out, have dinner, and go to a movie—and I like *made his day.* Well, anyway, today we passed in the hall between classes, I gave him a hard time about something stupid, and he just grinned.

It's way too beautiful a day to eat inside; gotta head outside for some sun. I know just the spot, a little grassy place right beside the library in the sun where the wall of the library blocks the wind. I'm gonna ask my buddy, Richard, if he wants to eat outside with me.

✳   ✳   ✳

Richard Castaldo was the first person shot and Rachel Joy Scott was the first person killed by Eric Harris and Dylan Klebold at Columbine High School on April 20, 1999.

Only Richard witnessed the final moments of Rachel's life. Rachel and Richard were sitting on the grass outside the Columbine library when Eric Harris and Dylan Klebold approached them.

Without warning, the two young men opened fire, severing Richard's spine and shooting Rachel twice in her legs and once in her torso. As Richard lay stunned and Rachel attempted to crawl to safety, the shooters began to walk away, only to return seconds later. At that point, Harris grabbed Rachel by her hair, held her head up, and asked her the question, "Do you believe in God?"

"You know I do," Rachel replied.

"Then go be with him," responded Harris before shooting her in the head.

Four bullets from Eric Harris's gun killed Rachel. He and Dylan then went into the school and aggressively, gleefully walked the halls of Columbine on a killing rampage.

Richard described Rachel's death to his mother in the initial days after the shooting, but has since blocked those details from his memory. Although Richard survived more than half a dozen gunshot wounds, he remains physically paralyzed and emotionally traumatized as a surviving victim of the most deadly school shooting in American history.

✳   ✳   ✳

From a Mother's Heart—

Dear Reader,

In the months since Rachel's death, I find it difficult to follow Christ's command to forgive the killers. Forgiveness is a daily choice for me. Sometimes it has even been a moment-by-moment struggle. From the beginning I have asked God to give me real forgiveness for Eric and Dylan, but that desire is repeatedly tested. The more knowledge I had about the two boys, the more violated I felt, and the more grace it took for me to walk in forgiveness.

Forgiveness for me is not a one-time act of my will, but it's a choice I make on an ongoing basis. I choose constantly to forgive, even when I don't want to, even when I don't feel forgiving. I choose constantly to lay down my pain because I trust that God is going to do something incredibly beautiful through all this.

My life has been about taking life as it comes, to make the best of whatever I've faced. And I've come through countless times of loss, transition, and change—times of beginnings and endings. But nothing could have prepared me for the loss of my daughter, Rachel Joy. As Rachel herself expressed, doing the right thing is hard, but it must be done. Knowing God forgave the killers of his Son, Jesus Christ, empowers me to rely totally on the grace of God to forgive the two young men who killed Rachel and the twelve other victims. Forgiveness is not based on how I *feel* on any given day. Forgiveness is a matter of choice.

Time magazine did an exhaustive twenty-page cover story about the killers after a reporter got access to five videotapes discovered in the boys' rooms. When the article was published right before Christmas, not even a year after Rachel's death, I cried for weeks. I felt so much anger and personal hurt knowing what the two young men had said on those videos. With the publication of that article and subsequent release of those videos came the painful awareness that Harris and Klebold specifically targeted Rachel. Klebold, who allegedly had a crush on Rachel, singled her out in the videos, calling her a "godly whore" and a "stuck-up little b****." When I found out that Rachel was on their target list, I struggled with my own anger, bitterness, and even hatred.

But again and again, I've chosen to bring my feelings of loss, sorrow, anger, and bitterness before the Lord, recognizing that *only* by God's grace am I able to forgive these two young men.

When Rachel's father and I talk to people around the country, we ask them to consider how a young man named Eric Harris and a young woman named Rachel Scott followed two opposite paths in their lives.

These two young people were born just days apart. They lived just a few miles away from each other. They died just minutes apart. But in many ways, they couldn't have been more different.

Eric Harris was a bitter, angry person who went out of his way to give voice to the inner darkness that governed his life. His Web site and videos made before the shooting are chilling evidence of one boy's hate.

Rachel's writings are at the opposite end of the spectrum. Repeatedly in her journals, she chose love, she chose compassion, and she chose to serve God with a passion.

Eric and Rachel both used the same phrase to describe what they were trying to do with their lives. Both talked about starting a "chain reaction."

For an assignment in one of her classes at Columbine, Rachel wrote a paper titled, "My Ethics, My Codes of Life." The paper clearly lists the core values Rachel held most dear: trust, honesty, compassion, love, and the desire to believe the best about people. She concluded her paper by saying: "My codes may seem like a fantasy that can never be reached, but test them for yourself, and see the kind of effect they have in the lives of people around you. You just may start a chain reaction."

In a video Eric recorded with Dylan Klebold before their rampage, Eric spoke of a quite different type of chain reaction. Through his actions on April 20, Eric hoped to kill hundreds of innocent students and thereby unleash terror and chaos.

Just about everybody gets picked on at school or in life, but those boys fed their hurts and insecurities until they became a powerful hate. They chose that hate, they thrived on it, and it burned within them like a smoldering fire.

Eric Harris probably didn't start out his life deciding he wanted to be a mass murderer. Rather, his life took shape step by step as he made decisions all along the way.

Neither did Rachel announce on her first birthday that she wanted to be a devoted disciple of Jesus Christ. Instead, it was through a series of fits and starts that she decided, over a period of years, to gradually give more and more of herself to God. Rachel encouraged others to make the best choices when they faced important decisions in their lives. She repeatedly encouraged her friends to consider the decisions of the present moment in the light of eternity.

Rachel had found a worthy cause, something she was willing to die for—but more important, something to *live* for. She realized that life, fulfillment, and meaning could only come through a relationship with Jesus Christ. Living her life with God's purposes at the very center—despite disappointment, hurt, struggles, fears, confusion, and questions—Rachel found an inner peace, a sense of direction, a consuming passion.

It is my desire that through the words Rachel wrote and the spirit of Rachel captured in this book, that you will come to understand that your whole life is based on the choices you make. Daily choices. Seemingly insignificant choices. My prayer is that you will make *good* choices—and the most important choice you make will be what you choose to believe about Jesus Christ. Make a choice for God, and God will become very real, very personal to you. god is not calling you to die for him but to live for him.

You don't have to be perfect to be used by the Lord. God does not use "perfect" people . . . because there aren't any! To be used by God just requires a willing heart, a desire for obedience to God's Word, and a love for God and others. Rachel had that desire, that love. And her life impacted everyone she met.

Can one life make a difference? Absolutely! Out of the horrible events and personal loss of April 20, 1999, Rachel's family, friends, and community of faith have come to experience what we call Columbine: Tragedy to Triumph. The ongoing story of the aftermath of that day is a challenge: *Who will pick up the fallen torch?*

I firmly believe that *you* are the one to pick up that torch. I don't think it is an accident or coincidence that you are reading this book. Something has drawn you to these pages, and something will move you beyond these words. I know that "something" is God working in your life. Although I may not know you personally, I am proud of you. I believe you have the courage and boldness to stand tall for your faith. You are part of a generation that has a great destiny in God's wonderful plan. I applaud you in every way. I encourage you to "pick up the torch."

In the mercy of Christ,
Beth Nimmo

i write . . .
for the sake
of my soul

eleven

the last word— rachel's writings

> I write, not for the sake of glory, not for the sake of fame, not for the sake of success, but for the sake of my soul.
>
> —Rachel Scott
>
> From the front cover of her last journal

Rachel's life on earth was ended prematurely by an act of violence. But the two shooters do not have the last word. Rachel would not have wanted to end this book with the events of her death. She would want the final word to be a word of life—and more than any other topic she covered, the words Rachel recorded are about life.

She wrote in a school assignment, "How do you know that trust, compassion, and beauty will not make this world a better place . . . test them for yourself, and see the kind of effect they have in the lives of people around you. You just may start a chain reaction."

Rachel would have wanted God to have the last word and that word is redemption. Rachel would have wanted this book to start a chain reaction, so the following essays, excerpts, and song lyrics written by Rachel are published here in the hope that you will make a choice to pay attention to the way in which God is working in your life—and in so doing, you just may start a chain reaction.

God gave Rachel a talent, a gift with words and creative expression, and *through her journals, poetry, songs, drawings, and dramatic activities, Rachel used those gifts for the glory of God. No matter what you do, no matter what you love to do—whether it's soccer or cooking, drawing or playing chess, singing or playing video games—buried somewhere in what you love to do most is a gift, a talent, God has given you. You have a choice . . . to let that gift be used for the glory of God or the glory of self. What you choose to do with what God has given you—is up to you.*

Wide awake

"Come on, Jake, get ready for school! Please, please, please try to get ready by yourself today," Jake's mom pleaded, gently shaking him.

Every morning since his grandfather died, Jake was unable to get up and get ready for school each morning. His mother would literally drag him out of bed and dress him. His father would brush his teeth and put him in the car. Once the car door opened at the school gate, he awoke as if just coming out of a dream.

Jake had loved his grandfather dearly. They were very close. His grandfather had taught him all he knew about God. Jake used to listen intensely, believing every word his grandfather said, but after he died, so did Jake's faith in God.

Jake decided to set out on a mission: to find God and know God the way his grandfather knew him. He asked people questions. He asked everyone, everyone except the new kid in class. He sorta became friends with the new kid—without ever talking to him. He saw him in the halls, and it seemed that this new kid was there every time Jake was in trouble. He always seemed to have a solution to every problem, and he helped without ever saying a word.

But Jake was doubtful. He had searched for proof. He had tried everything to find God. He had prayed, fasted, gone to church, sung songs, but nothing seemed to help him find his answer. Then things began to get worse. Jake found out that his best friend had a disease; he was missing a lot of school because he was having seizures. What little faith in God Jake still had was growing cold.

When things seemed hopeless to Jake, memories of his grandfather kept coming to mind. Missing his grandpa, he went into the den and sat down by the window in his grandfather's favorite chair. Quietly, half daydreaming, half praying, he imagined what he would say if his grandfather were still sitting in his favorite chair.

"Grandpa, how do you know there is a God?" he asked.

"Because Jake, I have proof," his grandfather said softly.

"What proof? Show me," he pleaded.

"The snow, Jake, nothing more than the snow on the ground. That is my proof. Everyone has their own proof and that is mine. You will have to find your own. It will come to you as a sign. Just when you think things are hopeless, call upon God and God will send you a sign," the grandfather replied.

Jake sat quietly in his grandfather's chair, warmed by the sunlight coming in the window as he remembered his grandfather's deep, slow voice and gentle, strong hands. Jake missed him more than ever. *God, I wish it would snow—Grandpa would've loved the snow.*

Jake took a deep breath, opened his eyes, and looked out the window—it was snowing! And he had asked God just moments ago to let it snow. It was his sign.

A few days later, Jake went up to the new kid and asked him his name.

"All this time you have seen me, and yet until now, you have never *really* seen me. I've been here, but you have never asked my name. Now that you know me, you will recognize me. You will know who I am," the new kid replied.

Jake turned for just a split second and when he looked back again, the kid was gone. In a split second, Jake had the answer that had been eluding him.

"I know two things for sure," Jake said. "One, God is real; and two, not all angels have wings."

✳ just between god and me

Look up the story in Luke 24:13–33 and read it a couple of times.

God is always present, always with us, giving us the chance to see with knowing eyes or look right past the obvious. The disciples on the road to Emmaus walked a long distance and talked at length with Christ, but didn't recognize him. Why? Were they too sad? Too preoccupied with everything that had happened?

Have you ever sought an answer to something, prayed about it over and over, and suddenly discovered the answer was right in front of you? In what ways has Jesus "made himself known to you"?

where love is . . . god is

"God, I read your Word, pray to you, and trust in you fully. I ask that you do with my life as you will and that you may use me to fulfill your every desire. Amen."

And so the old man went to sleep. He had a dream that night, a dream that Jesus came down and paid him a visit. The old man gave him tea to drink, food to eat, and a cloak for his bare arms.

"I will come to you tomorrow . . . look for me," Jesus told the old man. And then his Lord faded away.

The old man awoke, and for some reason, felt that this was more than just a dream. From the start of daybreak, the old man looked through his window, hoping to see Jesus.

As he sat watching for Jesus, he noticed a young man blowing his breath into his hands, trying to keep warm in the bitter cold. The old man invited him in and gave him some hot tea to drink. The young man drank the tea and regained his warmth. He thanked the old man and went back out into the cold.

The man began to pray and was deep in thought when he looked up, hoping to see his Savior, and noticed a beggar boy outside his window. He invited the boy in and gave the boy bread and butter for his thinning bones. The boy thanked the old man and went on his way with a full stomach.

It was later in the evening, when the wind had picked up to almost an unbearable howl, that the man again looked outside for Jesus. He found instead an old woman with a bundle in her arms leaning against the brick wall outside his home. He immediately asked her to come in before the wind blew her away. As she came in, the bundle began to cry, and the old man realized the woman was holding a baby. The baby was freezing and the mother was numb from the cold. He sat her down by the fire, went to his closet, pulled out his cloak, and wrapped it around her shoulders. He told her that when she was warm and the winds had died down, she would be able to go on her way. The woman pulled the cloak tightly around her, holding the baby close and quieting the baby's cry. When the wind had died to the barest whisper, she thanked the old man, stepped out into the still night air, and went on her way. The old man once again looked out his window, waiting, hoping, to see Jesus.

Perhaps another day, he thought. And he laid his head down to sleep. He looked around his small home and then noticed a figure in the corner.

"Step out to where I can see you."

The figure came into the light of the candle, and the old man recognized the young man he had brought in from the cold and given his tea to. Then the image changed, and it became the beggar boy who had eaten his bread and butter. The image then came to the old woman and her baby. It all smeared into bright light and the old man heard the voice of God.

"My faithful servant, my desires are their desires. My needs are met when theirs are met. When you love others . . . you love the Lord your God."

just between god and me

. . . .

. . . .

. . . .

. . . .

. . . .

. . . .

. . . .

. . . .

. . . .

. . . .

. . . .

. . . .

. . . .

. . . .

Most of us consider ourselves to be "honest people." We never "steal" or "lie." We do what is right. We are "truthful" to our loved ones. No one wants to be called a liar, but what makes a liar? We all lie, therefore, we are all liars. Some would disagree with that and say that there are exceptions. I have not found one. If we don't lie, we "improve the truth." For example, if your loved one came up to you with mismatched clothes, or messy hair, or a bad make up job, and asked you how they looked, you wouldn't tell them, "Unh... I'm not going out with you looking like that!" No, some would say, "You look nice dear." Others would say that they were not going to lie, but say something like, "Well, you do, but what would be even better is if you did this." Some would not call that a lie, but sensitivity. But wouldn't the brutal truth be, "You look like crap." Some would say that's just being mean. But what if the truth is mean? What if its not a pretty picture? Do you give it in all its harshness, or do you change it, even a little? People tend to "change," or "disguise," or "decorate" the truth, if not lie about it.

We would all rather hear the phrases "Sunset" and "sunrise." But the sun neither rises nor sets The TRUTH is that the world circles the sun. But how beautiful or romantic is that? You never hear songs or lyrics on how the earth circles the Sun. It's not pretty. So we change the truth and say the Sun rises and sets. Some say that there is nothing wrong with that. And there isn't. But that still doesn't make it the truth. It is still being decorated It is still a lie Anything but the harsh and brutal truth is a lie, an illusion. A picture you visualize in your mind, with a touch of beauty, instead of what's in front of your eyes. We would all prefer a beautiful lie over the cold truth. When a friend gets something you wanted, something small, something they didn't know that you wanted, you lie and pretend you are happy for them. Sometimes, we even convince ourselves that we are happy for them, only lying to ourselves. Deep inside of us (for some not too deep) we feel that we deserved the insignificant thing No matter what it is. We should have gotten it. We are more worthy or qualified for it. This is our truthful thinking, but we never say it.

And even if we do bring ourselves to tell the truth, usually, time has passed and it becomes resentment. In some cases, it can only be truthful, if it is known the moment it is thought. Sometimes the truth needs to be known instantly, instead of being hidden behind a "nice" lie. Otherwise, the truth is not in its wholeness and it is tainted with anger.

APOLOGIES FOR EXISTANCE

I'M SORRY...
I'M SORRY I COULDN'T BE
SMART ENOUGH FOR YOU.
AVERAGE is all I have to offer.

I'M SORRY...
I'M SORRY I COULDN'T BE
PRETTY ENOUGH FOR YOU.
AVERAGE is all I have to offer.

I'M SORRY...
I'M SORRY I COULDN'T BE
DESIRABLE ENOUGH FOR YOU.
AVERAGE is all I have to offer.

I'M SORRY...
I'M SORRY I AM WHO I ~~WAS~~ AM.
BUT THIS IS ALL I HAVE TO OFFER.

Just kickin' it with my buddy,

Just swingin' it with my pal,

The One who gave me life,

Is now the one I hang around.

Just talking to my Saviour,

Going over what we'll do,

'Bout to go out and tell the world

That Jesus loves them too.

Cause He is the One.

Who will fill the void inside,

He is the One.

Who will give eternal life,

He is the One.

Who will give undying love,

He is the One.

Who ~~will~~ reigns from Heaven Above,

He is the One.

Just lookin' at my heart,

Cryin' about all the pain.

Father, I am so sorry,

I am the only one to blame.

This burden upon my back,

Is tearing me apart.

Jesus come into my life,

Lord come into my heart.

Cause You are the One,

Who can fill the void inside.

You are the One,

Who gives eternal life.

You are the One,

Who gives undying love.

You are the one,

reigns from
Who ~~comes~~ Heaven above.

(ax's)

I gasp for air...   AAEE

Anybody out there?   EDC BCDA

Can anybody hear me?   CDC BCOE

Can anybody help me?   EFE DCD B

I'm drowning here...   AAEE

Losing my mind.   EDC BCDA

I'm dying here,   AA GA

Can't seem to find...   BBBC

Can't seem to find...   BBBA

I gasp for air .   AAEE

Anybody out there?   EDCBC DA

I don't want to die,   CDCBCOE

I don't like to cry.   EFE DCDB

But I'm drowning here...   AAEE

Losing my mind.   EDCBCDA

I'm dying here,   AAGA

Can't seem to find...   BBBC

Can't seem to find...   BBBA

Oh Father God...   AAEE *

Are You really out there?   EDCBCDA

Can You really hear me?   CDCBCDE

Can You really help me?   EFEDCDB

I'm drowning here...   AAEE

Losing my mind.   EDCBCDA

I'm dying here,   AAGA

Can't seem to find...   BBBC

Can't seem to find...   BBBA

Salvation.   AGA

Oh Father God...   AAEE

You are really out there!   EDCBCDA

You can really hear me!   CDCBCDE

You can really heal me!   EFEDCDB

Oh fill me up...   AAEE

Cleanse my mind.   EDCBCDA

Give me Your love,   AAGA

I have found You...   BBBC

I have found You...   BBBA

my Saviour.   AGA

just between god and me

Non-Profit
Rachel Joy Scott Memorial
1000 Englewood Parkway, Suite 3-302
Englewood, CO 80110
www.racheljoyscott.com

Speaking: Trinity Christian Center
6500 W Coal Mine Ave.
Littleton, CO 80123
(303) 979-3653
(303) 932-0378 Fax
Contact: Lynn Shotwell
tccdenver@aol.com

Ambassador Agency
PO Box 50358
Nashville, TN 37205
(615) 370-4700
(615) 661-4344 Fax
www.AmbassadorAgency.com